Contents

File on
STRINDBERG

Compiled by Michael Meyer

Methuen. London

A Methuen Paperback

First published in 1986 as an original paperback
by Methuen London Ltd,
11 New Fetter Lane, London EC4P 4EE
and Methuen Inc. 29 West 35th Street,
New York, NY 1001

Phototypeset in Times Roman
by Words & Pictures Ltd,
Thornton Heath, Surrey
Printed in Great Britain by
Richard Clay (The Chaucer Press) Ltd,
Bungay, Suffolk

British Library Cataloguing in Publication Data

File on Strindberg.—(Writer–Files)
    1. Strindberg, August—Criticism and interpretation
    I. Meyer, Michael, *1921–*   . II. Series
    839.7'26   PT9816

    ISBN 0 413 55020 6

Cover image based on a photo from the
BBC Hulton Picture Library

The theatre is, by its nature, an ephemeral art: yet it is a daunting task to track down the newspaper reviews, or contemporary statements from the writer or his director, which are often all that remain to help us recreate some sense of what a particular production was like. This series is therefore intended to make readily available a selection of the comments that the critics made about the plays of leading modern dramatists at the time of their production – and to trace, too, the course of each writer's own views about his work and his world.

In addition to combining a uniquely convenient source of such elusive *documentation*, the 'Writer–Files' series also assembles the *information* necessary for readers to pursue further their interest in a particular writer or work. Variations in quantity between one writer's output and another, differences in temperament which make some readier than others to talk and write about their work, and the variety of critical response, all mean that the presentation and balance of material shifts between one volume and another: but we have tried to arrive at a format for the series which will nevertheless enable users of one volume readily to find their way around any other.

Section 1, 'A Brief Chronology', provides a quick conspective overview of each playwright's life and career. *Section 2* deals with the plays themselves, arranged chronologically in the order of their composition: information on first performances, major revivals, and broadcasts is followed by a brief synopsis (for quick reference set in slightly larger, italic type), then by a representative selection of the critical response, and of the dramatist's own comments on the play and its theme.

Section 3 offers concise guidance to each writer's work (if any) in non-dramatic forms, while *Section 4*, 'The Writer on His Work', brings together comments from the playwright himself on more general matters of construction, opinion, and artistic development. Finally, *Section 5* provides a bibliographical guide to other primary and secondary sources of further reading and of collected editions of the plays.

The 'Writer–Files' series aim by striking this kind of balance between information and a wide range of opinion to offer stimulating and useful 'companions' to the study of a wide range of major playwrights in the modern repertoire.

1849   22 Jan., Johan August Strindberg born in Stockholm. Third surviving child of Carl Oscar Strindberg, a shipping agent, and his wife Nora, a former servant girl.

1853   His father goes bankrupt.

1862   His mother dies. The next year his father marries his housekeeper.

1867   Goes to Uppsala University to study humanities, but leaves after a term to teach at an elementary school and do private tutoring.

1869   Joins Royal Theatre of Stockholm as an actor, but fails. Writes his first three plays, *The Freethinker*, *A Nameday Gift*, and *Hermione*.

1870   Returns to Uppsala to study modern languages and political science. His fourth play, *In Rome*, is staged briefly at the Royal Theatre.

1872   Leaves Uppsala and settles in Stockholm. Writes his first major play, *Master Olof*, but it is not performed for nine years. Tries to become an actor again and fails again.

1872-74   Journalist in Stockholm.

1874-82   Librarian in Stockholm.

1877   Marries Finnish actress Siri von Essen.

1879   Establishes himself as an author with auto-biographical novel, *The Red Room*.

1880-82   Writes historical and pseudo-historical prose works; also *The New Kingdom*, a provocative volume of stories attacking the establishment, for which he is venomously attacked.

1883   Leaves Sweden (partly because of these attacks) to spend the next six years abroad in France, Switzerland, Germany, and Denmark. First real theatrical success with *Lucky Peter's Journey* (his ninth play).

1884   Publishes a volume of short stories, *Getting Married*; is prosecuted for blasphemy; returns to Sweden to face trial and is acquitted.

1886   Writes partly fictionalized account of his

childhood and youth, *The Son of a Servant*, and *The Comrades*, his first 'modern' play.

1887 Writes *The Father* in Bavaria: it has a small success in Denmark but fails in Sweden. Also writes rustic novel, *The People of Hemsö*, and, in French, *A Madman's Defence*, a malicious account of his marriage.

1888 Writes *Miss Julie* and *Creditors*, both in Denmark. *Miss Julie* is attacked on publication for immorality. Corresponds with Nietzsche.

1889 Starts his own experimental theatre in Denmark; *Miss Julie* and *Creditors* are staged there and fail. Theatre goes bankrupt. Strindberg returns to Sweden.

1890 *The Father* is staged at the Freie Bühne in Berlin, the first production of a Strindberg play outside Scandinavia.

1892 Divorces Siri. Writes *Playing with Fire* and *The Bond*, his last play for six years. Leaves Sweden for Berlin.

1893 Devotes himself for four years to science and painting. Marries Frida Uhl, an Austrian journalist. Visits England.

1894 Parts from Frida and settles in Paris. *Creditors* and *The Father* are staged there and are well received. Strindberg is lionised but makes little money.

1894-96 Continues in Paris with scientific experiments and theorizing; dabbles in the occult and alchemy and tries to make gold. Friendship with Gauguin, Munch, and Delius. *Inferno* crisis; hovers on brink of insanity.

1896 Emerges from mental crisis and returns to Sweden.

1897 Writes *Inferno* in French, an account of his years of near-madness.

1898 Writes Parts I and II of his dramatic trilogy, *To Damascus*. In the next eleven years he writes 35 plays.

1899 Writes *Gustav Vasa*, *There Are Crimes and Crimes*, and *Erik the Fourteenth*, his best historical play.

1900 Meets Norwegian actress, Harriet Bosse, 29 years his junior. Writes *Easter* and *The Dance of Death*, Parts I and II.

1901 Writes *The Virgin Bride*, *To Damascus*, Part III, and *A Dream Play*. Marries Harriet. She leaves him before the end of the year; returns briefly; then moves away for good.

1904-06 He writes no plays. Many of his best plays, such as

The Dance of Death and *A Dream Play*, remain unperformed. His reputation in Sweden goes into decline. But he is admired by his peers abroad, including Ibsen, Chekhov, Gorki, and Shaw.

1907   Founds his own Intimate Theatre in Stockholm. Writes four chamber plays for it: *Storm*, *A Burned House*, *The Ghost Sonata*, and *The Pelican*, the first three all within ten weeks. They are coldly received.

1909   Writes his last play, *The Great Highway*.

1909-12   Devotes last three years of his life to writing articles and pamphlets on politics, linguistics, and religion.

1912   14 May, dies in Stockholm of stomach cancer, aged 63.

This checklist inevitably contains much material from my biography of Strindberg (1985) and the introductions to my translations of the plays (1964, 1975). I should have liked to have been able to give more details of early US productions, but information on these is sparse and not always reliable. Most US productions in those days were pirated, and records of them do not exist; many were in Swedish and other languages by immigrant groups. All translations quoted are my own, except where otherwise specified.

Strindberg wrote 60 plays, of which less than a third are ever performed,or likely to be performed, outside Sweden. Even in Sweden, barely 30 are staged, except as curiosities. He was the most uneven of all great writers. He poured words onto paper day after day throughout his adult life; even when he abandoned creative writing for science for six years in the 1890s, he wrote copiously about that. His 60 plays form only a fraction of his total output (see page 49).

Success of a kind came to him early, but throughout his life it was his lesser plays which were acclaimed in Sweden, while his more ambitious works, the ones admired by posterity, tended to be rejected and ridiculed, though they won discriminating admirers abroad. He enjoyed a love–hatred relationship with the theatre; periodically he would abandon it for several years, return to it feverishly for a period, then abandon it again.

Strindberg was a theatrical pioneer in two respects. Firstly, in the late 1880s, when he was in his late thirties, he wrote a series of plays, notably *The Father*, *Miss Julie* and *Creditors*, which treated sex and marriage with a realism previously unknown in the theatre. Strindberg knew that people can fuck each other and hate each other; indeed, he believed that this was what sex and marriage were really about. This had been said by other writers in novels, but not in plays; in drama before Strindberg, fucking is done only by married people or wicked people. One has to use this verb when writing of Strindberg, because his characters do not make love; that is the tragedy of the couples in *The Father*, *Miss Julie*, and *The Dance of Death*.

Secondly, in his late forties and in his fifties, Strindberg wrote several plays, such as the *To Damascus* trilogy, *A Dream Play* and *The Ghost Sonata*, in which what most people call reality and fantasy merge, though Strindberg would have said that what most people call fantasy has a higher reality than what most people call reality. In this, he was the father of expressionistic drama and what is loosely known as the Theatre of the Absurd.

He also wrote a dozen historical plays, some of which are very fine; but the good ones are exclusively about Swedish personages little if at all known outside Scandinavia, and presuppose a background knowledge which no audience outside Scandinavia possesses. Whenever he wrote about an internationally known figure, such as Socrates, Luther, Charles XII or Queen Christina, he fell for some reason below his best.

Early Plays

In 1869, aged 20, Strindberg wrote two plays: *The Freethinker*, about a young teacher who loses his faith in Christianity, and a comedy, *A Nameday Gift* (which has not survived), about a conflict between a father and his son. *The Freethinker* contains the usual beginner's faults; everyone holds forth at length, and none of the characters except the hero has any real life. But it shows that even thus early Strindberg knew how to write dialogue. In 1870, he wrote two historical plays, *Hermione*, a melodrama set in ancient Greece, and *In Rome*, a verse comedy about the Danish sculptor Bertil Thorvaldsen, set around 1800. This slight piece was staged at the Royal Theatre in Stockholm and was sympathetically received, while *Hermione*, though unperformed, was praised by the Swedish Academy and published. Strindberg followed these in 1871 with a one-act prose play, *The Outlaw*, set in Iceland in the twelfth century, about a chieftain who is converted from paganism to Christianity. It was staged by the Royal Theatre and ill received, but won the admiration of King Charles XV, who awarded Strindberg a small stipend (which soon ceased). It is written in a pastiche of the formalized style of the Icelandic sagas, which clashed impossibly with Strindberg's modernity of outlook and naturally colloquial style. But it paved the way for his first great play the following year.

Master Olof

Historical prose drama in five acts.

Written: 1871-72, in Uppsala and Stockholm and on Kymmendö
in the Stockholm skerries. Rejected by the Royal Theatre and
rewritten, again in prose, in 1873-74. This was likewise
rejected, and Strindberg wrote a third version, in verse, in
1875-76, which suffered the same fate. The first version is by
far the best, and is the most frequently performed in Sweden.

First production: New Th., Stockholm, 30 Dec. 1881.

First British production: BBC Radio, 8 Jan. 1986 (dir.
Martin Jenkins; with Miles Anderson, Alfred Burke, and Dilys
Hamlett). Not staged to date in Britain or USA.

*The play is set in Sweden in the sixteenth century. Olof, a young
Swedish disciple of Luther, tries to introduce Luther's reforms
into Sweden and incurs the wrath of the established church. The
young king Gustav Vasa recruits him as a weapon against that
establishment, whose power he wishes to curb. But in his new
official position, Olof finds the king a tyrant against whom he
feels compelled to rebel as against the church, and when his
father-in-law Gert, a seasoned old revolutionary, plans to
assassinate the king, Olof joins the conspiracy. They are
discovered and condemned to death. Gert welcomes martyrdom
as the best way to advance the cause of radicalism, but Olof lets
himself be persuaded that he can achieve more as a living new
Luther (which, historically, he did). In a magnificent final
scene, a young disciple, ignorant that Olof has recanted, kneels
to him in the pillory and blesses him for choosing martyrdom,
while Gert, on his way to the block, cries the final word of the
play: 'Apostate!'*

Strindberg poured his own problems into the play: the dilemma of the
young who wish to revolutionize society and pull down what is old
and dead, yet who shrink from violence and a violent death. 'You
were born to make men angry', says one of the characters to Olof in
the opening scene. 'You were born to fight'. It is an unashamed self-
portrait.

'It is the story of my life.' (Strindberg, in a letter to Edvard Brandes,
29 July 1880)

'He [Olof] is no poetic Hamlet, but an angry man. It says so in the play. "The pale cleric", sharp in logic, thinks much, etc. "To fight with such a man required Satan himself!" And M.O. says of himself: "I have lived on a war footing and slept on my sword. And I had the strength to defy a world". Brazen – very young! He is as proud as a king. He is snappish, vitriolic and sullen. . . . Many have played your role, mostly like Hamlet. . . . Let us now see my Master Olof, our Luther! for the first time! . . . a man of cast iron with an extraordinary assurance who is not sympathetic and does not bother to be. Most actors have ended by playing him with warmth instead of fire. . . . His manner of speech is always arrogant, whether he is addressing bishop, king, or peasant'. (Letter to Ivar Nilsson, who was rehearsing the role, 16 Feb. 1908)

The rejection of *Master Olof* was not surprising. The qualities that make it admired today, the sharp modernity of its dialogue and characterization, were considered unsuitable in a play about ancient heroes. Poetry was still regarded as the only possible medium for stage tragedy, not only in Scandinavia but throughout the western world. The play lacked the declamatory monologues which audiences, and actors, expected, and the life-size quality of the famous historical figures bothered them; they wanted to see, and act, giants. The subtle relationships, too, needed the kind of acting which would emerge later in the century with Stanislavski and Duse.

Although Strindberg rewrote *Master Olof* twice in an effort to compromise with popular taste, first in prose and then in humdrum verse, the play had to wait nine years before it was staged, and then ironically in the original version. It was an experience with which Strindberg was to become increasingly familiar; several of his finest plays were to meet a similar, or worse, fate.

Discouraged, Strindberg wrote no more plays for four years, working as a journalist and librarian. In 1876-77 he wrote *Anno 48*, a political comedy set in Stockholm in 1848, the year of revolutions, a slight squib which seems only to have been performed once, in Germany in 1922. In 1879 he became famous through his first novel, *The Red Room*, and in 1880 wrote another play, *The Secret of the Guild*, set in Uppsala in 1401-02, dealing with the conflict between two master masons, one virtuous and one ruthless, both idealists in their own way, for the right of completing the city's cathedral. The Royal Theatre staged it immediately, but it was not a success and has seldom been revived.

In 1882 he wrote a 'five act saga play', *Lucky Peter's Journey*, a feeble imitation of *Peer Gynt* which Strindberg himself dismissed as a pot-boiler, and a period drama, *Sir Bengt's Wife*, the first of his plays in which the main part was a woman's. A knight rescues a girl from a convent and marries her, she is nearly seduced by another man, is saved by a father confessor, tries unsuccessfully to commit suicide, and is finally reunited with the knight. A terrible play, it yet contains the seeds of the great dramas which Strindberg was to write later that decade, for it is really a study of any nineteenth century marriage and its petty irritations. For the first time, he was writing about, not political, social or religious problems, but sexual relationships. The characterization is penetrative, but the plotting, and above all the final act, are feeble in the extreme. It was staged within months, but failed. *Lucky Peter*, by contrast, was acclaimed when staged the following year.

Knowing its true worth, Strindberg was cynical about this, his first popular success in the theatre, and abandoned drama for another four years. He spent this time in France and Switzerland, writing several volumes of short stories (one of which, *Getting Married*, resulted in his being tried for blasphemy, though he was acquitted), and several volumes of a partly fictionalized autobiography under the overall title of *The Son of a Servant*.

By now his marriage had begun to fall apart, and he, who had been extremely sympathetic towards female emancipation, now became violently anti-feminist. Although he denied that he was misogynistic, and said (which was true) that he could not live without women, his attitude towards them for the remainder of his life is often not easily distinguishable from misogyny. In 1886 he returned to playwriting.

The Comrades

Comedy in four acts.
Written: 1886-87, in Switzerland.
First production: Lustspielth., Vienna, 23 Oct. 1905.
First Swedish production: Intimate Th., Stockholm, 17 May 1910.
First London production: Everyman Th., 21 Feb. 1928 (dir. Malcolm Morley; with Pamela Carme, Sybil Arundale, and Ivan Samson). *Revived*: The Place (Royal Shakespeare Company), 10 Oct. 1974 (dir. Barry Kyle; with Susan Fleetwood, Rosemary McHale, and Peter Eyre). *Radio production*: as *Married Alive*; 26 Jan. 1951 (dir. Mary Hope Allen; with Lydia Sherwood, Judith Furse, and Griffith Jones).

First US production: Irving Place Th., New York, 1917 (dir. Rudolf Christians).

Set in contemporary Paris. A painter, Bertha, who wears a man's tie, has her hair short and smokes cigarettes, does not want to compromise her career by 'becoming a man's slave', but marries a fellow painter for economic reasons and also in the hope of curing her chlorosis, an illness caused by irregular menstruation. She has a painting accepted in a competition, while her husband's is refused. She tries in various ways to humiliate him until at length he sends her away and takes a mistress, revealing that the accepted painting is in fact his and that he had changed the numbers so as to provide his wife with a success. Other characters include an emancipated and bisexual woman named Abel, and Dr. Östermark, who was to reappear, like Bertha, in The Father.

Strindberg at first entitled the play *The Marauders*. He wrote three endings, two grim, one happy; none of them really works. For some reason, *The Comrades* enjoyed enormous success in Germany, where by 1927 it had received 1,174 performances, more than any other Strindberg play. In 1919 it was made into a German film, with Strindberg's third wife, Harriet Bosse, as Bertha.

'. . . subtle psychology, sceptical, irreverent, I'm afraid a bit improper'. (Letter to Verner von Heidenstam, 12 Aug. 1886)

'A comedy in 5 [sic] acts, the last 4 written in the past 8 days, which doesn't mean it's not good, because I can't write slowly'. (Letter to Albert Bonnier, 30 Nov. 1886)

'It may happen that my comedy will take off, if not this year then next (like *Ghosts*), and it will most assuredly be a monument or a milestone marking a stage in my literary development'. (Letter to Albert Bonnier, 31 Dec. 1886)

15

The Father

Tragedy in three acts.

Written: 1887, in Issigatsbühel, Bavaria, in two and a
half weeks.

First production: Casino Th., Copenhagen, 14 Nov. 1887.

First Swedish production: New Th., Stockholm, 12 Jan. 1888.

First London production: Pavilion Th., Whitechapel, 29 May
1911 (in Yiddish, for three performances during a visiting
season by the American Yiddish actor, Maurice Moscovitch).

First production in English: Rehearsal Th., Maiden Lane, 23 July
1911 (dir. Maurice Elvey; with Maurice Elvey and Alice Chapin).

Revived: Pavilion Th., Whitechapel, July, 1915 (in Yiddish; with
Maurice Moscovitch, Fanny Waxman, and Beckie Goldstein);
Everyman Th., 3 Aug. 1927 (dir. Milton Rosmer; with Robert
Loraine, Dorothy Dix, and Haidée Wright), trans. to Savoy
Th., 23 Aug. 1927; Everyman Th., 22 July 1929 ('reproduced'
by Douglas Ross, in modern dress; with Malcolm Morley,
Mary Grew, and Louise Hampton); Apollo Th., 14 Aug. 1929
(dir. Malcolm Morley; with Robert Loraine, Dorothy Dix, and
Louise Hampton); Pavilion Th., Whitechapel, Oct, 1931 (in
Yiddish; with Ben Zion Baratov); Grand Palais, Whitechapel,
29 Jan. 1942 (in Yiddish; with Mark Markoff and Eta Topel;
repeated for a few performances at Conway Hall, Bloomsbury);
Embassy Th., 30 Nov. 1948 (dir. Dennis Arundell; with
Michael Redgrave, Freda Jackson, and Lily Kann), trans. to
Duchess Th., 24 Jan. 1949; Arts Th., 20 Feb. 1953 (dir. Peter
Cotes; with Wilfrid Lawson, Beatrix Lehmann, and Nora
Nicholson); Piccadilly Th., 14 Jan. 1964 (dir. Casper Wrede;
with Trevor Howard, Joyce Redman, Gwen Nelson, Nigel
Stock, and Alfred Burke), trans. to Queen's Th., 3 Feb. 1964;
Old Vic Th., 24 Aug. 1971 (dir. Geoffrey Ost; with Wilfred
Harrison and Lorraine Peters); Th. Royal, Stratford East, 21
July 1976 (dir. Valerie Hanson; with Lee Montague and Rachel
Herbert); Open Space Th., Nov. 1979 (dir. Charles Marowitz;
with Denholm Elliott and Diane Cilento). *Television
productions*: ITV, 27 June 1957 (dir. Peter Cotes; with Basil
Sydney, Phyllis Calvert, and Mary Merrall); BBC, 21 Sept.
1962 (dir. Alan Bridges; with Robert Shaw, Daphne Slater, and
Wynne Clark); ITV, 4 Mar. 1968 (dir. Dennis Vance; with
Patrick Wymark, Dorothy Tutin, and Sybil Thorndike); BBC,
22 Sept. 1985 (dir. Kenneth Ives; with Colin Blakely, Dorothy
Tutin, Irene Handl, and Edward Fox). *Radio productions*:
4 Nov. 1946 (dir. Howard Rose; with Ralph Truman and Sonia

Dresdel); 21 Apr. 1952 (dir. E.A. Harding; with Robert Harris, Kathleen Michael, and Gladys Young); 31 Mar. 1957 (dir. John Gibson; with Jack Hawkins, Googie Withers, and Gladys Young); 25 Apr. 1972 (dir. John Tydeman; with Trevor Howard and Peggy Ashcroft).

First US production: Berkeley Th., New York, April 1912 (with Warner Oland and Rosalind Ivan).

Set in contemporary Sweden. Adolf, a cavalry captain, is driven by his wife, Laura, to suspect that their daughter Bertha (portrayed as an adult in The Comrades*) is not their child. He goes mad, tries to shoot Bertha, and is lured into a straitjacket by his old nurse. He has a stroke, and the play ends with us not knowing whether he will live or die.*

The Father should have been seen in London in the 1890s. J.T. Grein, the founder of the Independent Theatre, tells (*The Sketch*, 31 July 1929) how he 'tried in vain to cast it ... because all the women whom I approached to play the Captain's wife rebuffed me with the same answer: "You do not expect me to play that awful part?" '

It was Loraine's performance in *The Father* in 1927 which established Strindberg in Britain as a major playwright, but even this was surpassed by Lawson, whose interpretation has rightly become a legend. It remains the greatest individual Strindberg performance I have seen, in Britain or elsewhere. He was magnificently supported by Beatrix Lehmann. Trevor Howard was likewise masterly, in a fine production.

'The play can easily be destroyed and become ridiculous. ... A deceived husband is a comic figure in the eyes of the world, and especially to a theatre audience. He must show that he is aware of this, and that he too would laugh if only the man in question were someone other than himself. This is what is *modern* in my tragedy, and alas for me and the clown who acts it if he goes to town and plays an 1887 version of the Pirate King! No screams, no preaching! Subtle, calm, resigned! – the way a normally healthy spirit accepts his fate today, as though it were an erotic passion. . . . In particular, he symbolizes for me a masculinity which people have tried to pound or wheedle out of us and transfer to the third sex! [*a phrase Strindberg used when referring to feminists (as portrayed in* The Comrades*)*] It is only when he is with the woman that he is unmanly, because that is how she wants him, and the law of adaptation forces us to play the role that our sexual partner demands . . .'. (Letter to Axel Lundegård, 17 Oct. 1887)

'It seems to me as though I walk in my sleep – as though reality and imagination are one. I don't know if *The Father* is a work of the imagination or if my life has been; but I feel that at a given moment, possibly soon, it will cease, and then I will shrivel up, either in madness and agony, or in suicide. Through much writing my life has become a shadow-play; it is as though I no longer walk the earth, but hover weightlessly in a space that is filled not with air but with darkness. If light enters this darkness, I shall fall, broken.' (Letter to Axel Lundegård, 12 Nov. 1887)

Miss Julie

Naturalistic tragedy in one act (90 minutes).
Written: 1888, in Lyngby, Denmark (in two weeks).
First production: Copenhagen University Students' Union,
14 March 1889 (the planned première at Dagmars Th.,
Copenhagen, having been banned by the censor).
First public Swedish production: Academic Society, Lund,
18 Sept. 1906 (though a semi-private performance had taken
place at the Guildhall, Uppsala, in the spring of 1905). *First
performed in Stockholm*: People's Th., 13 Dec. 1906.
First London production: Little Th., 28 Apr. 1912 (with Octavia
Kenmore and Frederick Groves). *Revived*: the most notable
revivals have been: Arts Th., 13 Feb. 1933 (in French; dir.
Georges Pitoëff; with Ludmilla Pitoëff and George Pitoëff);
Arts Th., 27 Jan. 1935 (dir. Esmé Percy and Geoffrey
Dunlop; with Rosalinde Fuller and Robert Newton); Old Vic
Th., 8 March 1966 (dir. Michael Elliott; with Maggie Smith
and Albert Finney); The Place (Royal Shakespeare Company)
27 Oct. 1971 (dir. Robin Phillips; with Helen Mirren and
Donal McCann); Lyric Th., Hammersmith, 13 Jan. 1983
(dir. Clare Davidson; with Cheryl Campbell and Stephen
Rea), trans. to Duke of York's Th., 23 Feb. 1983.
TV productions: BBC, 23 Dec. 1956 (dir. Dennis Vance; with
Mai Zetterling, Tyrone Power, and Maureen Pryor); BBC,

3 Oct. 1965 (dir. Alan Bridges; with Gunnel Lindblom and Ian Hendry); BBC, 21 May 1974 (dir. Robin Phillips; with Helen Mirren and Donal McCann). *Radio productions*: 15 Sept. 1948 (dir. Peter Watts; with Joan Hart and John Carol); 13 Apr. 1959 (dir. Noel Iliffe; with Jill Bennett and Paul Daneman); 15 Jan. 1973 (dir. Betty Davies; with Janet Suzman and David Buck); 31 Dec. 1984 (dir. James Runcie; with Janet Maw and David Rintoul).

Filmed: at least five times in various countries, most notably in Sweden in 1950, a magnificent production by Alf Sjöberg, starring Anita Björk and Ulf Palme, which deservedly won the Grand Prix at the Cannes Film Festival of 1951.

Set in a country mansion in contemporary Sweden on Midsummer Eve. Julie, a Count's daughter, seduces her father's valet, Jean. They plan to elope, but this is frustrated by Jean's fiancée, the Count's cook Christine. Julie is revolted by what she has done, but knows she will want Jean again. Unable to bear that prospect, she commits suicide.

'Since they are modern characters . . . I have drawn my people as split and vacillating, a mixture of the old and the new. . . . My souls (or characters) are agglomerations of past and present cultures, scraps from books and newspapers, fragments of humanity, torn shreds of once-fine clothing that has become rags, in just the way that a human soul is patched together. . . . I have avoided the symmetrical, mathematically constructed dialogue of the type favoured in France, and have allowed their minds to work irregularly, as people's do in real life. . . .

'I have suggested many possible motivations for Miss Julie's unhappy fate. The passionate character of her mother; the upbringing misguidedly inflicted upon her by her father; her own character. . . . Also, more immediately, the festive atmosphere of Midsummer Night; her father's absence; her menstruation; her association with animals; the intoxicating effect of the dance; the midsummer twilight; the powerful aphrodisiac influence of the flowers; and, finally, the chance that drove these two people together into a private room – plus of course the passion of the sexually inflamed man. . . .

'Recently, people complained of my tragedy *The Father* that it was too tragic – as though tragedies ought to be jolly. One hears pretentious talk about "the joy of life". . . . I find "the joy of life" in life's cruel and mighty conflicts; I delight in knowledge and discovery. . . .

'On the question of technique I have, by way of experiment, eliminated all intervals. I have done this because I believe that our declining capacity for illusion is possibly affected by intervals, which give the spectator time to reflect and thereby withdraw from the suggestive influence of the author–hypnotist. . . . This form is by no means new, though it appears at present to be my monopoly. . . . If we could dispense with the visible orchestra . . . get rid of the side-boxes (my particular *bête noire*), with their tittering diners and ladies nibbling at cold collations, and have complete darkness in the auditorium during the performance; and, first and foremost, a *small* stage and a small auditorium . . . then perhaps a new drama might emerge, and the theatre might once again become a place for educated people'.

(Strindberg's Preface to *Miss Julie*, 1888)

'In France I always ate 5 lamb cutlets. . . . Each cutlet comprised half a pound of bone and two inches of fat, which I left. Inside sat a kernel of meat, *la noix*. I want to say to the dramaturg: give me the kernel!' (Letter to Georg Brandes, 29 Nov. 1888)

Miss Julie so shocked Strindberg's contemporaries that his publisher, Bonnier, rejected it, as did all the Swedish theatres. It had to wait eighteen years for its first professional production in Sweden. But it found discriminating admirers abroad: the Freie Bühne of Berlin staged it in 1892, and Antoine presented it at his Théâtre Libre in Paris in 1893. Chekhov recommended it to Gorki, who was equally enthusiastic. Its first fully successful production came in 1904, when Max Reinhardt, a great Strindberg pioneer (he directed no less than seventeen of his plays), staged it at his Kleines Theater in Berlin; it toured many cities, including Budapest. In Britain, it has probably been staged more frequently than any other foreign play, except perhaps *Hedda Gabler*, having received more than 40 professional productions since 1963.

Creditors

Tragi-comedy in one act (90 minutes).
Written: 1888, at Lyngby in Denmark (in two weeks).
First production: Dagmars Th., Copenhagen, 9 March 1889.
First Swedish production: Swedish Th., Stockholm, 25 March 1980.

First London production: Prince's Th., 10 March 1912 (with
Guy Standing, Miriam Lewes, and Harcourt Williams).
Revived: Arts Th., 20 Nov. 1927 (dir. Maurice Browne;
with Townsend Whitling, Ellen van Volkenburg, and Maurice
Browne); New Lindsey Th., 5 Feb. 1952 (dir. Philip Saville;
with Ferdy Mayne, Margaret Johns, and Philip Saville); Lyric
Opera House, Hammersmith, 3 March 1959 (dir. Casper
Wrede; with Michael Gough, Mai Zetterling, and Lyndon
Brook); Ashcroft Th., Croydon, 18 Nov. 1963 (dir. Terence
Kilburn; with Stephen Murray, Zena Walker, and Michael
Meacham); Open Space Th., 22 March 1972 (dir. Roger
Swaine; with Brian Cox, Gemma Jones, and Sebastian
Graham-Jones); New End Th., 21 Apr. 1980 (dir. Roy
Macready; with Malcolm Rennie, Heather Sears, and
Philip Bowen).
TV production: ITV, 10 Oct. 1972 (dir. Philip Saville; with
Kenneth Haigh and Susanna York).   *Radio productions*:
23 Jan. 1949 (dir. Wilfred Grantham; with Richard Williams,
Janet Morrison, and Sebastian Shaw); 21 Aug. 1972
(dir. Martin Jenkins; with Brian Cox, Gemma Jones, and
Sebastian Graham-Jones).
First US production: Stage Society, Boston, April, 1912.

---

*Set in a hotel on the west coast of Sweden in summer. Gustav, a
schoolmaster, formerly the husband of Tekla, a novelist, comes
to break up her new marriage to Adolf, an artist, and so revenge
himself on them both. The play comprises three dialogues:
between Gustav and Adolf, who does not know who Gustav is;
Adolf and Tekla, with Gustav listening; and finally, Tekla and
Gustav, with Adolf listening. The revelations he hears cause
Adolf, who is an epileptic, to have a fit; he dies, and Gustav's
mission is accomplished.*

'The plot is exciting, as spiritual murder must be; the analysis and the
motivation are exhaustive, the viewpoint impartial; the author judges
no one, he merely explains and forgives; and although he has made
even the promiscuous woman sympathetic, this does not mean that
he is advocating promiscuity. On the contrary, he says specifically
that it is a bad thing, because of the disagreeable consequences that it
brings.' (Letter to Joseph Seligmann, 29 Sept. 1888)

'It is a great favourite with me and I read it again and again, discovering new subtleties. . . . *Miss Julie* is still a compromise with romanticism. . . . but *Creditors* is modern right through.' (Letter to Joseph Seligmann, 16 Oct. 1888)

'. . . my most mature work. . . . You will find the vampire wife charming, conceited, parasitical (spiritual transfusion!), loving (two men at once!), tender, falsely maternal, in a phrase, woman as I see her!' (Letter to Charles de Casenove, 26 June 1892)

Not surprisingly, considering how far it was in advance of its time, *Creditors* took time to be appreciated, but it has since come to be regarded as one of Strindberg's most powerful plays. On the occasion of Casper Wrede's 1959 production at Hammersmith, one of the most effective Strindberg productions yet seen in Britain, T.C. Worsley wrote in the *Financial Times* of 'the richness and compression of this superbly taut, tense and terrible little play', and Milton Shulman in the *Evening Standard* declared: 'Strindberg's character delineation and barbed, incisive prose vibrate with a subtle intellectual power that has a fresh contemporary ring to it even after seventy years'.

The Stronger

Play in one act (15 minutes).
Written: 1888-89, at Holte in Denmark.
First production: Dagmars Th., Copenhagen, 9 Mar. 1889 (in a
    triple bill with *Creditors* and *Pariah*).   *First Swedish
    production*: by a touring company, 1903-04.   *First Stockholm
    production*: Intimate Th., 5 Dec. 1907.
First London production: Bloomsbury Hall, 29 Nov. 1906 (first
    production of any Strindberg play in Britain, for two
    performances only, by the New Stage Club; with Louise
    Salom and Millicent Murby).   *Revived*: His Majesty's Th.,
    10 Dec. 1909 ('The Afternoon Theatre'; with Lady Tree and
    Lydia Yavorskaia); Century Th., Bayswater, 15 June 1926
    (dir. Kate Rorke; with Shirley Bax and Chris Castor); Duke
    of York's Th., 21 Oct. 1931 (dir. Nancy Price; with Ethel
    Warwick and Nancy Price); Pembroke Th., Croydon, 16 Oct.
    1961 (dir. Basil Ashmore; with Margaret Rutherford and Jean
    Bloor); Orange Tree, Richmond, 11 July 1973 (dir. Brian Cox;

with Edith McArthur and Sheila Manahan); National Th. at the Cottesloe, 1 Dec. 1983 (dir. Roger Gartland; with Pauline Cadell and Judith Coke). *TV productions*: BBC, 22 Aug. 1958 (dir. Louis MacNeice; with Sheila Brennan and Yvonne Mitchell); ITV, 1 May 1971 (dir. Patrick Garland; with Britt Ekland and Marianne Faithfull).

First US production: Wisconsin Dramatic Society, Milwaukee, 1911.

A wife meets a woman friend in a café and, as she chats to her without reply, realizes that the friend is, or was, her husband's mistress.

'1. She is an actress, not just an ordinary respectable housewife. 2. She is the stronger, i.e. the softer. What is hard and stiff breaks, what is elastic gives, and returns to its shape.' (Letter to his wife, Siri, on how to play the wife, *c*. 6 March 1889)

Strindberg wrote three more plays in 1889: *Pariah*, *The People of Hemsö*, and *Simoom*.

Pariah, a 50-minute one-act play, is about two men, an archaeologist and an insect collector, both of whom have committed crimes in the past. The forger tries to blackmail the homicide, who, however, proves the stronger. An intellectually unconvincing piece, it offers powerful opportunities for a stage duel, but has not yet been staged in Britain except for a couple of performances in London on 11 Oct. 1927 (at 'Playroom Six'), as a curtain-raiser to *Miss Julie*. It has thrice been broadcast, in 1949, 1959 and 1962.

The People of Hemsö is a four-act adaptation which Strindberg made of his rustic novel of that name at the request of an actor–manager. Strindberg did the job reluctantly and always hated the play (though the novel is one of his best works), and was not surprised when it failed at its premiere. 'You see!', he wrote to the actor–manager, August Lindberg (5 June 1889), 'When one is untrue to oneself, the result is shit!'

Simoom is a 20-minute one-act melodrama about revenge set in a burial chamber in Algeria; an Arab maiden hypnotizes a French officer to death. A trivial piece, it was, with *The Stronger*, the first of Strindberg's plays to be staged in Britain (at the Bloomsbury Hall, 29 Nov. 1906), and perhaps the first to be staged in the USA, in 1905 at a private performance in the Vanderbilt mansion in New York.

Strindberg now turned his back yet again on the theatre, for three years. Then, in 1892, he wrote seven plays, five of them virtually worthless. *The Keys of Heaven* is a saga play like *Lucky Peter's Journey*, full of heavy-handed satire on Christianity, Swedish democracy, etc.; it had to wait 70 years for its unsuccessful Swedish premiere. *The First Warning*, *Debit and Credit*, and *In the Face of Death* (all one-acters) are equally devoid of merit.

Motherly Love, another one-actor, is not quite so bad. It shows a divorced woman, her feminist companion and her twenty-year-old actress daughter; the mother keeps her daughter isolated lest she should hear good of her father; the daughter finds her father to be a good man, but is unable to break free and remains the prisoner of the two older women. Like *The Comrades*, it contains excellent roles without being a convincing play. But later that year Strindberg wrote two interesting plays, *Playing with Fire* and *The Bond*.

Playing with Fire

Comedy in one act (75 minutes).
Written: 1892, at Dalarö, in the Stockholm skerries.
First production: Lessingth., Berlin, 3 Dec. 1893 (dir. Max Reinhardt).
First Swedish production: 3 May 1907, at a *soirée* in the National Restaurant, Stockholm (dir. Mauritz Stiller, later a famous film director and the director of Greta Garbo).
First London production: Aldwych Th. (Royal Shakespeare Company) 18 June 1962 (dir. John Blatchley; with Michael Hordern, Sheila Allen, and Kenneth Haigh); Open Space Th., 7 Nov. 1972 (dir. Peter Watson; with Celia Bannerman, Allan Surtees, and Gabrielle Blunt). *TV production*: ITV, 13 June 1970 (dir. Gareth Davies; with David Cook, Mel Martin, Vivien Heilbron, and Michael Mackenzie). *Radio production*: 31 Aug. 1960 (dir. H.B. Fortuin; with Nigel Stock, Mary O'Farrell, Perlita Neilson, and Peter Woodthorpe).

Set on the west coast in contemporary Sweden. Six people are on summer holiday, all except the old mother lusting after someone not their rightful partner. Axel, a young man in the throes of divorce, becomes infatuated with Kerstin; when they tell her husband, he agrees to release her provided she and Axel agree to marry. But Axel does not want to rush into another marriage and when Kerstin becomes hysterical he leaves; whereupon she and the others sit down to lunch.

Playing with Fire is a black comedy, and shows Strindberg at his wittiest (an aspect of his genius which is often overlooked). The chief reason that the Swedish premiere was so long delayed was, according to his daughter Karin, that the characters were so obviously and libellously based on former friends of his, a painter Robert Thegerström and his family, that no theatre or publisher would consider it. Strindberg had visited the Thegerströms at Dalarö the summer before he wrote the play, but had quarrelled with them and had taken this spiteful revenge, as he was to do with his own sister and her husband in *The Dance of Death*. The plot was also partly based on Strindberg's experience with his wife Siri von Essen (whom he was then divorcing) and her first husband, Baron von Wrangel, seventeen years earlier, when Wrangel, like Kerstin's husband in *Playing with Fire*, was in love with his cousin and was willing to let his wife enjoy herself elsewhere.

The Bond

Tragedy in one act (80 minutes).
Written: 1892, at Dalarö, in the Stockholm skerries.
First production: Kleines Th., Berlin, 11 Mar. 1902 (dir. Max Reinhardt; with Emmanuel Reicher and Rosa Bertens).
First Swedish production: Intimate Th., Stockholm, 31 Jan. 1908.
Not yet staged in Britain. *Radio production* (as *The Link*): 18 Oct. 1953 (dir. Frederick Bradnum; with Peter Coke, Isabel Dean, and Mark Dignam).

Set in a courtroom in contemporary Sweden, and based partly on Strindberg's divorce hearings on Värmdö in the Stockholm skerries a few months earlier, partly on Siri's divorce from her first husband, Wrangel, in 1876. The antagonists are, like Wrangel and Siri, a Baron and Baroness; each wants custody of the child. The title refers to the child, echoing an exchange in The Fathers, *when Laura asks: 'Why didn't we part in time?', and the Captain replies: 'Because the child bound us; but the bond became a chain'.*

The rejection of *Playing with Fire* and *The Bond*, together with the other works which Strindberg had written this year, caused him to abandon the theatre yet again, and for six years he wrote no plays. After his divorce from Siri, he went abroad, to Germany. He made a second marriage, with a 21-year-old Austrian journalist, Frida Uhl, but it soon failed, and he settled in Paris, devoting himself exclusively to science and the occult. He became especially interested (as many people did at that time) in alchemy, and made repeated attempts to make gold. He underwent a spiritual crisis, described in his book *Inferno* (which he wrote in French). That he survived this was largely due to his discovery of the writings of his compatriot, the mystic Emmanuel Swedenborg, which taught him that suffering was not meaningless but was a sign that, like Christ, the sufferer was one of God's elite.

In 1898 he returned to Sweden and, after writing *Inferno* and its sequel, *Legends*, took up playwriting again, to such effect that in the six years from 1898 to 1903 he wrote no less than 26 plays, including several of his finest. Most of these were realistic (thirteen were historical); but he also attempted a new genre, in which reality and fantasy merge. The most notable examples of this genre are the *To Damascus* trilogy, *A Dream Play*, and *The Ghost Sonata*.

To Damascus

Prose trilogy: Part 1 in five acts, Part 2 in four acts, and Part 3 in a single act of nine scenes.

Written: Part 1 was planned in Paris in 1898. It and Part 2 were both written in Lund in 1898, Part 3 in Stockholm in 1901.

First production: Part 1, Dramatic Th., Stockholm, 19 Nov. 1900; Part 2, Lorensberg Th., Gothenburg, 9 Dec. 1924; Part 3, Lorensberg Th., Gothenburg, 16 Nov. 1922.

First London production: Part 1, Stage Society, Westminster Th., 2 May 1937 (dir. Carl H. Jaffé; with Francis James, Wanda Rotha, and Tristan Rawson). Parts 2 and 3 have not been staged in London, nor has Part 1 been revived, but on 3 and 5 April 1975 the three parts were staged at the Traverse Th., Edinburgh (dir. Mike Ockrent and David Gothard; with Roy Marsden, Katharine Schofield, and Ron Forfar): Part 1 was presented on some nights, Parts 2 and 3 together on others; and on selected nights, all three parts were given, in a performance lasting five hours. This production was rightly acclaimed: Allen Wright in the *Scotsman* summed it up as 'a play so packed with ideas and invective that it makes most contemporary dramas seem trivial'. *Radio productions*: 13, 15, and 19 Dec. 1953 (dir. Peter Watts; with Valentine Dyall and Catherine Salkeld); 4 and 11 July 1971 (dir. Charles Lefeaux; with Stephen Murray and Zena Walker). This latter production was very fine.

First US production: Auditorium, New York, 1914 (with Ralph Winter).

Part 1

A famous writer in 'a strange city' feels damned and persecuted. He meets an unhappily married woman and takes her away from her husband, but lacks the money to support her and is humiliated by having to seek help from her relatives. He has an accident and wakes in a monastery which is also a madhouse; here his feelings of guilt become living figures, people whom he has injured in the past. His mother-in-law, a pious Catholic, explains that these torments are a necessary part of the process of salvation; he must be humbled, like Saul on the road to Damascus. Gradually and unwillingly he comes to accept that his fate is directed by a benevolent, if stern, power.

Strindberg constructed *To Damascus*, Part 1, like a circle. The Stranger passes through seven stations before reaching the asylum, then returns to each of them in reverse order to end on the street corner where he began. Several of the scenes reflect episodes from his second marriage with Frida Uhl.

When Strindberg wrote Part 1 in the spring of 1898, he had no thought of writing a sequel, but during the summer he began Part 2. With characteristic inconsistency, he made it less forgiving and resigned than Part 1.

Part 2

The Stranger's marriage is already on the rocks. While his wife is in the pangs of childbirth, he, preoccupied with his scientific research, finds a letter which she has intercepted confirming that his efforts to make gold have been proved successful and offering him membership of the Academy and a decoration. The next scene is at the Academy banquet, with the Stranger as the guest of honour; some diners are in full evening dress, some strangely in suits, and some are dressed as tramps. The better-dressed diners leave and he finds himself with only the tramps, who insult him. The barmaid demands payment from him for the banquet, since he is the only member left. Unable to pay, he is taken to prison, where he finds himself sharing a cell with a Beggar who is his double. Released, he hurries back home, where he is amazed to find that the child is not yet born. He asks: 'Can it take so long? . . . How is the mother?', to which his mother-in-law replies: 'The same as she was when you left a minute ago'. Everything that we have seen in the last two scenes has taken place in his mind, aroused by a suspicion that his wife may *have intercepted a letter to him. He goes to a whore to degrade himself ('Dirt hardens the skin against the thorns of life'), but even she will not have him. Finally, the Beggar reveals himself to be the Dominican who had received him in the abbey-asylum – 'your terrible friend', says the Lady, 'who has come to collect you'. As she cradles their baby, he is tempted to stay with her instead of going to the monastery, as he knows he must if he is to find peace. The final words of the play are: 'Come, priest, before I change my mind.'*

Two years later, early in 1901, when he had fallen in love with Harriet Bosse, Strindberg began Part 3 of *To Damascus*. He seems to have completed most of it that February, but added to it during the summer and autumn, by which time he had married Harriet and she had left him, returned to him and left him again.

Part 3

Part 3 opens with the Stranger at the foot of the mountain on which the monastery stands. He meets people, including his own son, who are suffering from syphilis, which they have contracted as a result of listening to the Stranger's exhortations to reject conventional morality. The Lady, who at the beginning of the play was his second wife, now becomes successively his mother

*and his third wife. He returns to society and remarries his
second wife, but that soon ends. He sees his first wife with a new
husband. His disillusionment with women is now complete, and
he enters the monastery, where his old self is symbolically buried
and he is re-baptized with a new name 'like a little new-born
child'. Parts 1 and 2 are the work of someone who has found a
kind of peace. Part 3 is the bitter lamentation of a man who has
been deprived even of that.*

'Herewith a play – I have no inkling of its worth. If you find it good,
chuck it in at the theatre. If you find it impossible, hide it away.'
(Letter to Gustaf af Geijerstam, 8 March 1898, enclosing Part 1)

'The fact was that a kind of religion had developed in me, though
I was quite unable to formulate it. It was a spiritual state rather than
an opinion founded upon theories, a hotch-potch of impressions that
were far from being condensed into thoughts. . . . In my boyhood I
had borne the Cross of Jesus Christ, but I had repudiated a God who
was content to rule over slaves cringing before their tormentors.'
(*Inferno*, trans. Mary Sandbach (Harmondsworth: Penguin, 1979),
p. 125, 181)

'My crisis of nearly seven months has not made me any more certain
except on some points. . . . Alchemy and occultism, looking into the
future and probing the occult, are completely forbidden, but not
speculative chemistry. On the other hand, I seem to have regained the
grace of being able to write for the theatre . . . a gift which can be
taken from one if one misuses it. As regards religion, I have had to
stop at a moderately warm connection with the beyond, which it
seems one may not approach too intimately, or one will be punished
with religious fanaticism and led astray. But I am not sure whether it
is a temptation to be withstood or a call to be obeyed.' (Letter to Axel
Herrlin, 10 Mar. 1898, two days after finishing Part 1)

'In 1867 Renan and Taine and Zola (Darwin was no atheist) began
this flouting of the Powers. . . . But now the return of the Powers is
approaching, now people light candles and seek God. . . . Those who
probed through arrogant inquisitiveness too deeply into forbidden
secrets such as the occultists (and I) saw more than they wanted to

and the Sphinx rent them one after the other. But occultism led men back to an understanding of God and the certainty that there are others who control our destinies. That is the standpoint that I have reached, and I have reached no further, but it seems to me that with the return of the Powers there return old demands, for order and discipline, etc. I even believe that the old morality will return, but with much stronger demands.' (Letter to Waldemar Bülow, 1 Apr. 1898)

'I have several times ground to a standstill in my new play [Part 2]. Decided to burn it, as totally worthless, although I'm near the end of Act 4. But I'm going on. It is conceived in hatred and deals with hateful people. Although it's strongly constructed and has a number of good things in it, it upsets me and makes me ill.' (Letter to Emil Kléen, 9 July 1898)

'I long for cleanness, beauty and harmony. Act 2 of *To Damascus* is influenced by B[osse] who has now entered my life.' (Strindberg's diary, 11 Feb. 1901)

Advent

Tragedy in four acts.
Written: in Lund, 1898.
First production: Kammerspiele, Munich, 28 Dec. 1915. *First Swedish production*: Dramatic Th., Stockholm, 22 Jan. 1926.
First London production: Old Vic Th., 12 Dec. 1921 (dir. Robert Atkins; with Rupert Harvey, Gladys Dale, and Ernest Milton). *Revived*: Bedford Hall, Chelsea, 1929 (dir. Pax Robertson).

Set in contemporary Sweden. An unjust judge and his malignant wife come to see the evil of their ways. Like To Damascus, *Advent combines realism with fantasy, sometimes with powerful effect. When the judge unwittingly invokes the Devil, the latter appears as a poor schoolmaster with a red neckerchief and carrying a cane. There is a macabre ball, at which musicians with chalk-white faces play, and the judge's wife finds herself partnered by a hunchbacked prince who abuses her. In the final act, the wife freezes to death in a marsh, while the judge is stoned to death by people whom he has unjustly condemned. They meet in hell where, it being Christmas, each is given a peepshow in which they see their past life, even love appearing as 'two cats on an outhouse roof'. At this moment of greatest humiliation, the advent star shines. Knowledge of their guilt has cleansed them and given them hope of redemption.*

Realism and fantasy are not as skilfully blended as in *To Damascus*, and the didacticism to which Strindberg was always prone sometimes intrudes uncomfortably. The play is not often performed, even in Sweden; but I have seen it work powerfully on the stage. It is a play that deserves greater attention than has been given to it, though it needs tremendous presences in the two main roles, and in several of the minor ones.

'Herewith the Mystery in the spirit of Swedenborg. Never have I been so unsure whether I have succeeded or failed. No idea whether it is good or awful.' (Letter to Gustaf at Geijerstam, 19 Dec. 1898)

There Are Crimes and Crimes

'Serious comedy' in four acts.
Written: in Lund, 1899.
First production: Dramatic Th., Stockholm, 26 Feb. 1900.
First British production: Playhouse, Oxford, 7 Mar. 1927, as
    Intoxication, presumably translated from the German title for
    the play, *Rausch*. Many of the early Strindberg 'translations'
    were made from German or French (dir. Claud Gurney; with
    Glen Byam Shaw, Margaret Webster, Alan Napier, and
    Alan Webb).
No London stage productions to date, or TV productions.   *Radio
    productions*: 14 May 1929 (dir. Howard Rose; with Michael
    Hogan and Gladys Young); 9 Feb. 1951 (dir. Wilfred
    Grantham; with Godfrey Kenton and Betty Baskcomb);
    12 Feb. 1962 (dir. H.B. Fortuin; with Kenneth Griffith and
    Joan Greenwood).

Set in contemporary Paris. A dramatist, Maurice, living with his common-law wife Jeanne, has a success with a play, falls in love with a sculptress, Henriette, and wishes his little illegitimate daughter dead so that there will be no obstacle to his marrying Henriette. The child dies, Maurice is arrested on suspicion of murder, his play is withdrawn, and his friends turn against him. It transpires, however, that the child died a natural death. He returns to public favour and gives up Henriette, but Jeanne will not forgive him, and the play ends with him going into a church, like the Stranger at the end of Part 1 of To Damascus, *to settle his conscience with God.*

There Are Crimes and Crimes is an attempt to breathe new life into French boulevard drama, that genre which Strindberg so despised. *To Damascus* and *Advent* had failed to interest the theatres, and he needed to be performed. The play works well in its way until the last act, when it falls apart; but, like *Lucky Peter's Journey*, it was to succeed in the theatre where so many of his best plays were rejected or failed.

'Now I am writing another play; an all too human drama, in which all the people are angels and do the most horrible things – just as in life. The villains are too cunning to break the law.' (Letter to his daughter Kerstin, 1 Feb. 1899)

'*Crimes and Crimes* seems to have been a great success but it brings me no joy.' (Strindberg's diary, 1 March 1900, shortly after the première). One can understand his disillusionment at the success of this pot-boiler when *To Damascus* had been rejected and *Miss Julie* remained unperformed in Sweden.

The Saga of the Folkungs

Historical drama in five acts.
Written: in Lund, 1899.
Unperformed to date in Britain and the USA.

Set in Sweden during the fourteenth century. It tells the story of Magnus the Good, the last of the Folkung dynasty, King of Sweden from 1319 (when he was three years old) until 1365, the first man to be ruler of both Sweden and Norway. When the play opens, all is well with Sweden; the Russian invaders have been expelled, the slaves freed, laws have been passed establishing human rights, and Magnus is hailed as the 'saviour and prince of peace'. He recognizes this as hubris, and the nemesis he dreads descends on him in full measure. His wife betrays him, his son plots to replace him, revolt threatens, he is excommunicated, and the Black Death reaches the land. Finally, the people depose him in favour of his son. Magnus, like Shakespeare's Henry VI, is portrayed as a good man but an ineffectual monarch; he sees himself as one destined to suffer for the sins that others have committed.

The Saga of the Folkungs is a splendidly powerful and vivid play, with strongly realized characters and magnificent crowd scenes; and, like Strindberg's other historical plays, it is virtually unknown outside Scandinavia. For some reason, Strindberg later disowned it; on 12 Aug. 1905 he wrote to Emil Schering: 'The play is among the worst constructed that I have written, and the characters weak'. But he did not feel thus when he finished it, and at once began the first of two even better sequels. It was a great success at its premiere, as it was when recently revived in Sweden in 1975 and 1979.

Gustav Vasa

Historical drama in five acts.
Written: in Lund, 1899.
First production: Swedish Th., Stockholm, 18 Oct. 1899.
Not yet performed in Britain.
First US production: Chicago, 22 Jan. 1912 (in Swedish).

Set in sixteenth century Sweden. Gustav Vasa has been king for ten years; the fiery young revolutionary portrayed in Master Olof *has become the father of his people, a mixture of benevolence and ruthlessness, merciless towards former friends and allies who have turned against him. He does not enter until Act 3, but his presence dominates all that goes before. The final act shows him facing what seems to be an irresistible revolution, ready to give up and flee the land; but he is saved by a force from the province of Dalecarlia which he thinks has come to the aid of the rebels, but which has come to suppress them. Master Olof, meanwhile, has changed even more than his king and become a skilful politician, an obedient servant of his master, and a devious spinner of webs; he tells his son: 'When I was your age, I thought I knew and understood everything. Now I know nothing and understand nothing, so I limit myself to doing my duty and patiently enduring.'*

Gustav Vasa is one of Strindberg's finest historical plays, though sadly his presupposition of background knowledge would render it scarcely comprehensible to a foreign audience. It was enthusiastically received when staged, Strindberg's first commercial success in the theatre since *Lucky Peter's Journey* fifteen years earlier. Within four months he was to have two more commercial successes in *Erik the Fourteenth* and *There Are Crimes and Crimes*.

'Formerly, I used to tell everything in the beginning [of a play], now I hold back secrets and thereby keep the interest all the way through, and have a surprise for the last act. You may remember that my first acts were always praised. ... That was a mistake, for I was too hot-headed and fired away so furiously that all my powder was expended by Act 3.' (Letter to Gustav af Geijerstam, 7 Jan. 1899)

Erik the Fourteenth

Historical drama in four acts.
Written: at Furusund, in the Stockholm skerries, and in Lund, 1899.
First production: Swedish Th., Stockholm, 30 Nov. 1899.
Not yet staged in Britain or the US. *Radio production*: 24 Dec. 1972 (dir. Martin Jenkins; with Alan Dobie and Lee Montague).

Set in sixteenth-century Sweden. The epileptic and deranged Prince Erik, memorably portrayed in Gustav Vasa, *has succeeded to the throne. He hates the nobles who effectively rule the land and, under the influence of his plebeian counsellor, Göran Persson, imprisons their leaders and then, in a fit of rage, has them murdered. There is a rebellion, led by Erik's two brothers, and he is deposed. The play ends with him fleeing with his peasant mistress, Karin Månsdotter, whom he has just married, into the night.*

Erik the Fourteenth is not only Strindberg's best historical play, but one of his most powerful works. Instead of a hero as its protagonist, as in *Gustav Vasa*, it has an epileptic failure, and its somewhat impressionistic method makes it seem extraordinarily modern today. Erik, unlike Gustav Vasa, was a character with whom Strindberg could identify; like Shakespeare, he knew that medieval kings were often hysterical weaklings.

The play is virtually unknown outside Scandinavia for the same reason as Strindberg's other historical plays – a presupposition of background knowledge which no foreign audience possesses. Every Swedish schoolchild knows that Erik was ultimately imprisoned and murdered; it is as though an English play about Charles I were to end with him as Cromwell's prisoner but confident of success. It is a marvellous final curtain for anyone who knows the outcome, but would leave a non-Scandinavian audience bewildered. Yet a little ingenuity can overcome the problem; all that is needed is a couple of impersonal explanatory sentences spoken in a black-out after the play's conclusion. The play worked admirably when broadcast in English in 1972.

Erik the Fourteenth received two notable productions in Sweden during the 1950s. In 1950, the great Alf Sjöberg directed it excitingly in Stockholm with Ulf Palme as the King and Lars Hanson as Göran Persson, and in 1956 Ingmar Bergman staged it equally excitingly, though quite differently, in Malmö, with Toivo Pawlo as the King, Åke Fridell as Göran, and three rising players – Bibi Andersson, Max von Sydow, and Ingrid Thulin – as Karin, Duke Charles, and the whore, Agda. In 1954 Sjöberg made a brilliant film based on the play entitled *Karin Månsdotter*, with Jarl Kulle as the King, Ulf Palme as Göran, and Ulla Jacobsson as Karin.

In 1899-1900, Strindberg wrote *Gustav Adolf*, about the seventeenth-century warrior king who was the nephew of Erik XIV and the father of Queen Christina. It is an immense piece, some six hours long; piqued by accusations of inaccuracy in his earlier plays, Strindberg researched it minutely, clotting it with undramatic detail which blurs the many fine scenes it contains. He concentrated the action into the last two years of the king's life, when success in the Thirty Years War has begun to sour. Its political complexities are scarcely comprehensible and it has seldom been staged. He followed it with a 'religious comedy' (as he termed it), *Midsummer*, one of his feeblest works, and *Casper's Shrove Tuesday*, a short puppet play; as the puppet master goes off to find some paint to smarten his puppets up, they pop up from their box and fight. It reads slightly, but I have seen it done with puppets to make an enchanting half hour.

Easter

'Passion play' in three acts.
Written: in Stockholm, 1900.
First production: Schauspielhaus, Frankfurt-am-Main, 9 Mar. 1901.
First Swedish production: Dramatic Th., Stockholm, 4 Apr. 1901.
First London production: Bedford Hall, Chelsea, 19 Mar. 1922 (dir. Pax Robertson). *Revived*: Arts Th., 10 Oct. 1928 (dir. Allan Wade; with Gwen Ffrangcon-Davies, Peggy Ashcroft, and Colin Keith-Johnston); Grafton Th., 28 May 1933 (dir. G.R. Schjelderup); Gateway Th., 30 March 1945 (dir. Basil Ashmore; with Esmé Percy); Hampstead Th., 18 Oct. 1965 (dir. Desmond O'Donovan; with Meg Wynn Owen and Victor Henry). *Radio productions*: 27 Mar. 1938 (dir. Peter Cresswell; with Gwen Ffrangcon-Davies, Marius Goring, and Robert Farquharson); 29 Mar. 1948 (dir. Peter Watts; with Louise Hampton, Valentine Dyall, and Allan Jeayes); 23 May 1954 (dir. Wilfred Grantham; with Betty Hardy, Anthony Jacobs, and Elizabeth Henson).
First US production: Little Th., Chicago, 1 Feb. 1913 (in Swedish).

Set in contemporary Sweden, in a small provincial town (clearly Lund) between Maundy Thursday and Easter Eve, when nothing happens and nothing is heard from the street outside save the scraping of the creditor's stick and the squeaking of his galoshes. Mrs. Heyst lives with her son and daughter, the son's fiancée, and a schoolboy lodger, under the shadow of her husband's imprisonment for embezzlement. The son, Elis, is suspicious and bitter; his sister Eleonora has run away from a mental hospital where she has been confined. They dread the coming of the creditor, but when he arrives in the final act he turns out to be not the monster of their imagination, but a kindly man who feels in debt to them.

Easter is a very still play, the forerunner of those 'chamber plays' which Strindberg was to write for his own Intimate Theatre seven years later. Elis himself is very much a self-portrait, of the arrogant, self-centred, and intolerant husband that Strindberg knew himself to be. He must be positive and rebellious, like the Stranger in *To Damascus*, not passive. Eleonora needs to be very carefully cast; she must be innocent without being mawkish, an elusive combination to attain; and she too must be positive, not passive. She must have, as Charles Morgan wrote in his *Times* review of the 1928 London production, 'the fire that gives light to the symbol'.

'We die continually that we may have continual resurrection. This is Strindberg's answer. He states it with extraordinary emphasis, with the passion of conviction. But is it the passion of a conviction that he has forced upon himself? Is his answer made thus, not because a truth within him would not allow it to be made otherwise, but because he could no longer bear to stay answerless? Is this the reason that the play, for all its high theme, its nobility of approach, its courage in inquiry, is never moving? There is a flaw in it somewhere. By the standard of *The Father* it is cold. ... The truth seems to be that Strindberg's desperate swerving towards orthodoxy yielded him an answer that was still no answer for him.' (Charles Morgan, *The Times*, 1 Dec. 1928)

The Dance of Death

'Marriage drama': Part 1 in four scenes, Part 2 in three scenes.
Written: in Stockholm, 1900.
First production: Altes Stadttheater, Cologne, 29 and 30 Sept. 1905.   *First Swedish production*: Intimate Th., Stockholm, 8 Sept. and 1 Oct. 1909.
First London production: Sunday Players, St. George's Hall, 23 Nov. and 21 Dec. 1924 (dir. George Merritt; with George Merritt, Sybil Arundale, Sylvia Willoughby, and Colin Keith-Johnston).   *Revived*: Part 1, Gate Th., 30 Nov. 1925 (dir. Peter Godfrey; with George Merritt, Molly Veness, and Peter Godfrey); Part 1, Apollo Th., 16 Jan. 1928 (dir. Robert Loraine; with Robert Loraine, Miriam Lewes, and Edmund Gwenn); Old Vic. Th., 21 Feb. 1967 (dir. Glen Byam Shaw; with Laurence Olivier, Geraldine McEwan, and Robert Stephens); Aldwych Th., 15 June 1978 (Royal Shakespeare Company; dir. John Caird; with Emrys James, Sheila Allen,

Lynsey Baxter, and Anton Lesser). Riverside Studios, Hammersmith, 30 May 1985 (dir. Keith Hack; with Alan Bates, Frances de la Tour, and Anne Louise Lambert). A notable production of Part 1 took place at the Royal Exchange Th., Manchester, 15 Sept. 1983 (dir. Kenneth Macmillan; with Edward Fox and Jill Bennett).

TV productions: ATV, 7 March 1966 (dir. John Moxey; with Paul Scofield, Mai Zetterling, Judy Geeson, and Barry Justice). *Radio productions*: 12 Apr. 1953 (dir. Donald McWhinnie; with Michael Hordern, Beatrix Lehmann, Marcia Ashton, and Cyril Luckham); 30 Jan. 1961 (dir. H.B. Fortuin; with Donald Wolfit, Margaret Leighton, Sebastian Shaw, and Catherine Dolan); 4 June 1972.

First US production: T. Lister's company, 1912. *Revived*: Theatre Guild, New York, 1920 (with Albert Perry and Helen Westley).

Part 1

Set in contemporary Sweden. Unlike Easter, *which is a play of reconcilation and hope,* The Dance of Death, *Part 1, written in the same month with no thought of a sequel, is an expression of the blackest pessimism and hatred. An army captain, Edgar, and his wife Alice, have been married for 25 years and hate each other. She was an actress who gave up her career for marriage. They are visited by Kurt, her cousin; he pities her and is attracted by her. But he finds her to be as evil as Edgar, and leaves them to continue on their treadmill. The final speech of the play ends: 'Blot out the past and go on living. Well. Let's go on.'*

Strindberg at this time depended much on German productions for his income, and when his German translator, Emil Schering, told him on receipt of Part 1 that he feared it might be too pessimistic to sell, Strindberg, the following month, wrote Part 2, in which the children of the characters in Part 1 seek the happiness which eluded their parents.

Part 2

Edgar's daughter Judith and Kurt's son Allan fall in love. Edgar wants to marry her for his own sake to a sixty-year-old colonel, and gets Allan transferred to a regiment in Lapland, but Judith sends the Colonel a rude telegram which makes him break off the engagement and arranges to join Allan. Edgar has a stroke; he speechlessly spits in Alice's face and she strikes him. But when he dies, she says: 'I see him now as he was when he was twenty. I must have loved that man. . . . And hated him. Peace be with him.'

Part 2 is a less effective play than Part 1, though it has a splendid final scene and Judith is a rewarding role. There are inconsistencies which make it difficult to stage the two parts together (Edgar, impoverished in Part 1, has unexplainedly become affluent in Part 2), and they are seldom staged together in Sweden. Part 1 works better by itself, and lasts two and a half hours, which is enough for any evening. Loraine, following his performance in *The Father* the previous year, was magnificent in the role. Laurence Olivier achieved a great success with it, though he hardly answered Strindberg's demand for 'ugliness, age, and whisky' (see below); Emrys James was closer to Strindberg's conception. Another memorable interpretation of the role was that by Erich von Stroheim, in a film which he directed (in French, in Italy) in 1947; unfortunately, he had a very weak Alice.

' "The Dance of Death, my boy! That's my best play!" Strindberg often repeated. . . . "The Captain! What a part!" And he jumped up and acted it for me. "A refined demon! Evil shines out of his eyes, which sometimes flash with a glint of Satanic humour. His face is bloated with liquor and corruption, and he so relishes saying evil things that he almost sucks them, tastes them, rolls them around his tongue before spitting them out. He thinks of course that he is cunning and superior, but like all stupid people he becomes at such moments a pitiful and petulant wretch".

'And with sweet-sour expressions, with gestures both jaunty and pathetic, he walked around or threw himself in a chair. What he particularly liked to act was the powerful scene when Alice, with a bored expression, plays the march "The Dance of the Boyars", which incites and hypnotizes the Captain to dance – wildly and clumsily, terrifyingly. At such moments [Strindberg] was an excellent actor – a great dramatic talent. His vivid impersonation remains for ever in my mind's eye and echoes in my ears.' (August Falck, *Fem år med Strindberg* (Stockholm, 1935), p. 282-3)

'First and last, the Captain must look old. His ugliness, age, and whisky must be visible.' (Letter to August Falck, 8 Aug. 1909)

'Strindberg's power of *creating* character is so great that you accept his monstrous originals more readily than the faithful copies of lesser dramatists. The unnatural and direful elements are so mixed in Edgar and Alice that we proclaim them not the recognizable men and women of our world, but logical and consistent inhabitants of the world devised in Strindberg's tortured brain. . . . The curtain has not been up ten minutes before we perceive that we are not dealing with falsification of the familiar, but with a different kind of new truth. If we could be translated to another planet, we should not be on that planet ten minutes, I suggest, without perceiving that its inhabitants were consistent with themselves, and that that consistency was not impaired by what we had hitherto known of sentient beings. So it is with Strindberg.' (James Agate, *Sunday Times*, 22 Jan. 1928)

The Virgin Bride

Drama in five scenes with Epilogue, also known in English as
   The Bridal Crown.
Written: in Stockholm, 1900-01.
First production: Swedish Th., Helsinki, 24 Apr. 1906. *First
   Swedish production*: Swedish Th., Stockholm, 14 Sept. 1907.
Not yet staged in Britain. *Radio production*: 24 Nov. 1974
   (dir. Martin Jenkins; with Martin Jarvis and Sarah Badel).
First US production: Experimental Th., New York, Feb. 1938.

Set in the countryside of Dalecarlia, Sweden, in the middle of the nineteenth century. Two peasant families are about to settle a long-standing feud through the marriage of the son of one family to the daughter of the other. But Mats and Kersti, unknown to the parents, are already lovers and have a baby. Kersti, without Mat's knowledge, gives the baby to a midwife to dispose of so that she may appear at her wedding wearing a virgin's crown. As they dance at the wedding feast in the mill, Kersti's crown falls into the millrace, and in the ensuing search the baby's body is discovered. Kersti is condemned to life imprisonment. In an unconvincing Epilogue, often omitted in performance, Kersti is drowned and the families are reconciled.

The idea for the play may have arisen from Strindberg's feelings of guilt about his first child with Siri, Kerstin, born three weeks after their marriage. Writing to his cousin Oscar ten years later, Strindberg said she was 'taken home by the midwife and died there two days after her birth'. The mother in the play is named Kersti. He may have written the play for his daughter Greta, who had recently made her debut as an actress and who played Kersti many times before her death in 1912. *The Virgin Bride* is one of Strindberg's finest plays, though it is virtually unknown outside Scandinavia. Ingmar Bergman directed a memorable production of it at Malmö in 1952.

'The play ... is an attempt by me to enter into Maeterlinck's wonderful world of beauty, leaving aside analyses, questions and standpoints. I know that I have only stopped at the entrance; I must burn the rubbish in my soul to be worthy of entry'. (Letter to Harriet Bosse, 8 Feb. 1901). Strindberg was much excited at this time by Maeterlinck. He translated part of Maeterlinck's collection of essays, *The Treasure of the Humble*, and planned also to 'translate, publish and stage' him in Sweden (letter to Gustaf Brand, 9 Feb. 1901), but this plan came to nothing.

After the brilliant period from 1898 to January 1901, in which Strindberg wrote seven of his best plays, he wrote five lesser works in rapid succession: *Swanwhite*, *Charles the Twelfth*, *To Damascus, Part 3*, *Engelbrekt*, and *Christina*.

Swanwhite is a sentimental piece, influenced by Maeterlinck's early play *The Princess Maleine*; a princess loves and is loved by a young prince and, when he drowns, recalls him to life by the purity of her love. *Charles the Twelfth* deals with the last three years of the life of the young eighteenth-century warrior king who unsuccessfully invaded Russia, was imprisoned in Turkey, and was killed, possibly by one of his own men, when besieging a fortress in Norway. Like so many of Strindberg's lesser works, it starts well but fades. *To Damascus, Part 3*, has already been described (see p. 28). *Engelbrekt*, about the leader of a fifteenth-century peasant rebellion, has no merits. *Christina*, the daughter of Gustav Adolf who abdicated and became a Catholic, contains a fat leading role but little else.

Alone among these five plays, *Christina* still enjoys some life in Sweden; a monarch who abdicates exercises a peculiar hold on popular imagination. But it is a poor piece. *Swanwhite* was broadcast by the BBC in 1949 and 1954; *Christina* was briefly performed by the Stage Society in London in 1937 and was broadcast in 1954 (with Yvonne Mitchell). Neither *Charles the Twelfth* nor *Engelbrekt* has been performed in Britain, nor have any of these five plays received anything but minor productions in the USA. But Strindberg ended this otherwise disappointing year with one of his most remarkable dramas.

A Dream Play

'Dramatic lyrical-fantasy' in fourteen scenes (part prose, part verse).

Written: in Stockholm, 1901.

First production: Swedish Th., Stockholm, 17 Apr. 1907.

First London production: Chelsea Arts Th., 1930 (dir. Pax Robertson).

Revived: Grafton Th., 2 Apr. 1933 (dir. G.R. Schjelderup; with Donald Wolfit, Natalie Moya, Richard Goolden, and George Merritt); Lyric Players Th., Belfast, 28 Feb. 1973 (dir. Donald Bodley; with Pitt Wilkinson, Kathleen McClay, and John Franklyn); Traverse Th., Edinburgh, 2 May 1974 (dir. Mike Ockrent; with Simon Callow and Roy Marsden), revived 21 Aug. 1974 for the Edinburgh Festival; Royal Shakespeare Company, Barbican Th., London, 3 July 1985 (dir. John Barton; with Penny Downie, Roger Allam, and George Raistrick). *Radio productions*: 22 Nov. 1948 (dir. Peter Watts; with Valentine Dyall and Molly Rankin); 17 June 1982 (dir. Martin Jenkins; with Dennis Quilley, Frank Finlay, Ian Richardson, and Lynsey Baxter), an outstanding production. London has also seen two foreign productions: by the Th. am Kurfurstendamm, Berlin, at Sadlers Wells Th., 21 June 1957 (dir. Oscar Fritz Schuh), and by the Dramatic Th. of Stockholm at the Aldwych Th., 19 Apr. 1971 (dir. Ingmar Bergman).

First US production: Provincetown Players, New York, Jan. 1926.

As Strindberg states in his preface (see below), the play moves freely in time and space. The daughter of the God Indra is sent to earth as a mortal, Agnes, to find the reasons for humanity's misery. She meets an officer imprisoned in a castle; visits an opera house where the officer comes to meet his love, who never appears as he grows older and older; marries a poor man's lawyer, has a child and experiences the toils of marriage; is set upon and beaten, and finally puts off her earthly form to return to heaven.

'In this dream play, the author has, as in his former dream play, *To Damascus*, attempted to imitate the inconsequent yet transparently logical shape of a dream. Everything can happen, everything is possible and probable. Time and place do not exist; on an insignificant basis of reality, the imagination spins, weaving new patterns; a mixture of memories, experiences, free fancies, incongruities, and improvisations. The characters split, double, multiply, evaporate, condense, disperse, assemble. But one consciousness rules over them all, that of the dreamer; for him there are no secrets, no illogicalities, no scruples, no laws. He neither acquits nor condemns, but merely relates; and, just as a dream is more often painful than happy, so an undertone of melancholy and of pity for all mortal beings accompanies this flickering tale.' (Strindberg's prefatory note to *A Dream Play*)

'In what land of dreams I am living, I know not, but I dread descending again to reality.' (Letter to Harriet Bosse, 13 Mar. 1901, a week after their engagement)

'Life becomes more and more dreamlike and inexplicable to me. Perhaps death really is the awakening.' (Letter to Carl Larsson, 2 Nov. 1901, two weeks before Strindberg finished *A Dream Play*)

'Am reading about Indian religions. The whole world is but a semblance. . . . The world has come into existence only through Sin – if in fact it exists at all – for it is really only a dream picture (consequently my *Dream Play* is a picture of life), a phantom, and the ascetic's allotted task is to destroy it. But this task conflicts with the love impulse, and the sum total of it all is a ceaseless wavering between sensual orgies and the anguish of repentance. This would seem to be the riddle of the world. . . . Indian religion, therefore, showed me the meaning of my *Dream Play*, and the significance of Indra's Daughter, and the Secret of the Door = Nothingness. Read Buddhism all day.' (Strindberg's diary, 18 Nov. 1901, the day he finished *A Dream Play*)

In 1902-03, Strindberg wrote six plays, only the first of which is of any quality. *Gustav the Third* is about the eighteenth-century Swedish king who, though an autocrat, found much to admire in the French Revolution, founded the Swedish Academy and the Royal Theatre, and was assassinated by a revolutionary at a masked ball (as portrayed in Verdi's *Un Ballo in Maschera*). This was someone with whom Strindberg could identify, and the result was one of his best plays; but, like his other histories, it presupposes a background knowledge which few non-Scandinavians possess.

The Dutchman is a curious fragment about an eternal wanderer who returns as always after seven years at sea in his perpetual and ill-fated attempt to find 'reconciliation through woman'. He meets and marries a young girl, but they prove incompatible and she leaves him, as Harriet had recently left Strindberg, thirty years her senior; at this point, Strindberg abandoned the play.

The Nightingale of Wittenberg deals with Luther; it opens intriguingly with Luther, as a schoolboy, being visited in his parents' home by a scholar who turns out to be Dr. Faustus, but the rest of the play hardly lives up to this, and the character of Luther does not really develop.

Strindberg then conceived the ambitious plan of writing a 'world-historical' drama about key figures of history, and within six weeks completed three plays, about Moses, Socrates, and Christ, entitled *Exodus*, *Hellas*, and *The Lamb and the Beasts* (the beasts being the emperors Caligula, Claudius, and Nero). Even Strindberg never wrote worse plays than these, and he seems to have realized it, for he does not appear to have offered them to a publisher or a theatre, and they have been very rarely performed. Written in many short scenes, their characterization is rudimentary and their dialogue archaic; they are neither good history nor good drama. He then abandoned drama for three years and wrote two patchy novels, *The Gothic Rooms* and *Black Banners*.

In 1906 he decided to start another experimental theatre, despite the failure of his earlier attempt in Denmark two decades previously. He put a young actor-manager, August Falck, who had just successfully staged the first professional Swedish production of *Miss Julie*, in charge, and in 1907 wrote four 'chamber plays' for it. Strindberg's scheme was partly inspired by Max Reinhardt's experiment in Berlin with a tiny auditorium, and partly by Maurice Maeterlinck's chamber plays such as *The Blind* and *The Uninvited Guest*, with their avoidance of conventional plot and conflicts and concentration on the inward dialogue which remains unspoken and which we sense behind and between the lines – what Maeterlinck called *la tragédie immobile* and *le théâtre statique*.

In a letter to Adolf Paul (6 Jan. 1907), advising Paul on how to write his next play, Strindberg wrote: 'Seek the intimate, a small theme exhaustively treated, few characters, big viewpoints, free imagination, but built on observation, experience, closely studied; simple but not too simple; no elaborate apparatus, no superfluous minor characters, no conventional five-acters or "old machines", no drawn-out "whole" evenings. *Miss Julie* (without an interval) has stood the test of time here and shown itself to be the form desired by this impatient age; searching but short!' This was an exact description of the plays which he was to write for his Intimate Theatre, and of which *Easter* had been a forerunner.

Storm

Chamber drama in three scenes (80 minutes).
Written: in Stockholm, 1907.
First production: Intimate Th., Stockholm, 30 Dec. 1907.
First British production: Bristol Express Company, Heriot-Watt
  Th., Edinburgh, 18 Aug. 1978 (dir. Andy Jordan; with Jim
  Smith, Laura Davenport, and Jenny Seagrove).   *Radio
  production*: 27 Sept. 1953 (dir. Mary Hope Allen; with
  Paul Rogers, Edward Chapman, Rosalie Crutchley, and
  Maxine Audley).
First US production: Irving Place Th., New York, 1916.

Set in contemporary Stockholm. It is summer and the city is empty; the Gentleman sits alone, waiting for death: 'I have settled my account with life, and have already begun to pack for the journey'. A former singer moves into the apartment above; his wife Gerda turns out to be the Gentleman's ex-wife, much younger than he. They meet and talk of the past. The singer elopes with an eighteen-year-old girl, taking his and Gerda's child; the elopement fails, Gerda regains her child and leaves her husband, and, this brief disturbance over, the Gentleman sits down again to await death. 'Let our memories be put to bed and sleep in peace. The peace of old age. This autumn I shall leave this silent house.' It is a subtle and astringent study of resignation and a marvellous role for an old actor.

'. . . a painful poem with which I wanted to write you and our child out of my heart.' (Letter to Harriet Bosse, *c.* 7 May 1908)

Strindberg followed *Storm* with another chamber play, *The Burned House* (also known in Britain and the USA as *After the Fire*), about an old man who returns to Sweden from America to find that his childhood home has burned down. Talking to neighbours and seeing objects that have survived, he finds his rosy memories of childhood replaced by uncomfortable truths, and returns saddened and wiser to the world outside. It is less successful than *Storm*, consisting of a lengthy monologue interwoven with some rather melodramatic and unconvincing sub-plots. But Strindberg followed it with one of his most powerful and daring plays.

The Ghost Sonata

Chamber drama in three scenes (90 minutes).
Written: in Stockholm, 1907.
First production: Intimate Th., Stockholm, 21 Jan. 1908.
First British production: Playhouse, Oxford, 15 Nov. 1926 (dir.
  J.B. Fagan; with Elliott Seabrooke, Veronica Turleigh, Glen
  Byam Shaw, and Alan Webb).   *First London production*:
  Globe Th., 14 June 1927 (dir. J.B. Fagan; with Allan Jeayes,
  Mary Grey, Glen Byam Shaw, and Alan Napier).
TV productions: BBC, 16 March 1962 (dir. Stuart Burge; with
  Robert Helpmann, Beatrix Lehmann, Ann Bell, and Jeremy
  Brett); BBC, 23 March 1980 (dir. Philip Saville; with Donald
  Pleasance and Lila Kedrova).   *Radio production*: 23 Oct. 1955
  (dir. Frederick Bradnum; with Cyril Shaps, Betty Hardy, and
  Allan McClelland).
First US production: Provincetown Players, New York, 1924.

A student, Arkenholz, meets an old man in a wheelchair, Hummel, who befriends him. Arkenholz has second sight; he sees a milkmaid whom no one else sees, and his mention of her terrifies Hummel, who long ago murdered her. Through a window of a house they see a beautiful girl; Hummel says she is his illegitimate daughter and that he can arrange for Arkenholz to meet her. That evening they enter the house, the mistress of which is the girl's mother, who sits in a cupboard and talks like a parrot, and is known as the Mummy. Hummel accuses those who live in the house, except his daughter, of crimes, which he says he will expose so that his daughter and Arkenholz can start life afresh here. But the Mummy in turn accuses Hummel; he crawls into her cupboard and hangs himself. In the final scene, Arkenholz confesses his love to the daughter, but she is tainted like everybody else in the house and dies. Arkenholz's last words over her body are: 'Unhappy child, born into this world of guilt, suffering and death, this world that is for ever changing, for ever erring, for ever in pain. The Lord of Heaven be merciful to you on your journey.'

'I am sending you today a second Chamber Play (opus 3) called *A [sic] Ghost Sonata* (subtitled Kama-Loka, though that needn't be printed) [*Kama-Loka is a kind of ghost or dream world through which mortals, or some mortals, have to wander before they enter the peace of death's kingdom*]. It is horrible like life, when the veil falls from our eyes and we see things as they are. It has shape and content; the wisdom that comes with age, as our knowledge increases and we learn to understand. This is how "The Weaver" weaves men's destinies; secrets like these are to be found in *every* home. People are too proud to admit it; most of them boast of their imagined luck, and hide their misery. ... What has saved my soul from darkness during this work has been my religion. ... The hope of a better life to come; the firm conviction that we live in a world of madness and delusion (illusion) from which we must fight our way free. For me things have become brighter, and I have written with the feeling that this is my "Last Sonata".' (Letter to Emil Schering, 27 Mar. 1907)

'Now I am assuredly entering into something new. I long for the light, have always done so, but have not found it. Is it the end that is approaching? I don't know, but I feel that it is so. Life is, as it were, squeezing me out, or driving me out, and I have long since rested all my hopes on "the other side", with which I am in contact (through Swedenborg). A feeling has also come over me that I have completed my work, that I have nothing more to say. My whole life often seems to me to have been planned like a play, so that I might both suffer and depict suffering.' (Letter to Emil Schering, 2 Apr. 1907)

The Ghost Sonata was attacked and ridiculed when first staged, and (as with so many of Strindberg's plays) it was Max Reinhardt who first revealed its possibilities, at his Kammerspiele in Berlin in 1916. The same year he took his production to Sweden, where it created a considerable sensation.

It was Strindberg's last great play, perhaps even his last good one. His last chamber play, *The Pelican*, is a heavily melodramatic piece about a widow who starves her grown-up children and flirts with her son-in-law; he, on finding that the dead man left nothing, loses interest in her. The son lights the stove to get some warmth and sets the apartment on fire; the mother throws herself from the balcony while the son and daughter die contentedly in the flames.

In 1908-09, Strindberg wrote three Swedish historical plays, *The Last Knight* and *The Protector*, both set in the sixteenth century in Gustav Vasa's youth before he became king, and *The Earl of Bjälbo*, about the thirteenth-century ruler Birger Jarl; also a play for children, *Abu Casem's Slippers*, and a Christmas play, *The Black Glove*, both in humdrum verse; and, finally, *The Great Highway*, another verse drama about a huntsman who has gone into the mountains to rediscover his soul, returns to humanity, and is involved in various encounters culminating in a meeting with a blind woman in a dark forest.

None of these plays is of much value, though they contain the odd nugget, and they are very rarely revived even in Sweden. Strindberg then abandoned the theatre for the last time and devoted his remaining three years to writing about politics, linguistics, and religion.

Strindberg was an immensely prolific writer, and his sixty plays form only a fraction of his total output; the definitive edition of his work now being prepared in Sweden will fill some 75 volumes. He wrote five full length novels, *The Red Room*, *The People of Hemsö*, *By the Open Sea*, *The Gothic Rooms*, and *Black Banners*; eleven volumes of partly fictionalized autobiography under the overall title of *The Son of a Servant* (*The Son of a Servant*, *Time of Ferment*, *In the Red Room*, *He and She*, *The Author*, *A Madman's Defence*, *The Monastery*, *Inferno*, *Legends* – these last two, like *A Madman's Defence*, in French – and *Alone*); several short novels, such as *Tschandala*, *The Romantic Organist of Rånö*, *The Roofing Ceremony* and *The Scapegoat*); and over 150 short stories, the best of which are to be found in the collections entitled *Swedish Destinies and Adventures*, *Getting Married* and, especially, *Men of the Skerries*. Apart from *The People of Hemsö*, a delightful but virtually untranslatable story of life in the Stockholm skerries, Strindberg's novels are very uneven, lively dialogue scenes alternating with dull didactic stretches; this is equally true of his 'autobiographical' books, except *Time of Ferment* and *Inferno*. He wrote several volumes of poetry, of variable and generally moderate quality (nor was he a good dramatic poet), and collections of equally variable essays on history, sociology, science, politics, linguistics and religion (to name only a few subjects), as well as the curious miscellany, *A Blue Book*. He also left a remarkable *Occult Diary*, of which only fragments have been published in English to date, and over 8,000 letters.

3: Non-Dramatic Writing

'A desolate longing for his mother stayed with him all his life. . . . He never became himself, he was never liberated, never a complete individual. He remained a mistletoe that could not grow without being supported by a tree. . . . He came frightened into the world and lived in perpetual fear of life and people.'

(Strindberg of himself in *The Son of a Servant*, 1886)

'To work all day so as to be able to eat, and then to eat so as to be able to work all the next day, is a horrible circle. Poverty makes a man . . . petty and mean – there's no broad view of the world from a rubbish heap.'

(Letter to Eugène Fahlstedt, 18 Apr. 1875)

'I am quick to attack but then my humanity intervenes and I grieve at having struck my fellow mortals, even if they have deserved it. So I cannot be a trusty friend nor a constant enemy. . . . As you see, I am a bad person to know! . . . A few words about my political beliefs. . . . I am a socialist, a nihilist, a republican, anything that is anti-reactionary! . . . I want to turn everything upside down to see what lies beneath; I believe we are so webbed, so horribly regimented, that no spring-cleaning is possible, everything must be burned, blown to bits, and then we can start afresh.'

(Letter to Edvard Brandes, 29 July 1880)

'I don't want to go with anybody; I want to be angry when I have cause, to go mad when my heart bids me, to climb over barricades and tread forbidden territory when the desire takes me and I feel young, I want music, I want the right to walk in the countryside, to love my wife and children, to keep my naive belief in God, I want to be free!'

(Letter to Professor C.R. Nyblom, 24 Jan. 1882)

'For me the theatre is omega. . . . You know how one has to lie once the curtain is up and how little one is allowed to say. The theatre is a clique set-up for Stockholmers and scripts don't get read unless you write like Ibsen and we can't do that.'

(Letter to Pehr Staaff, 3 July 1883)

'God, how I've been abused! And the things they say! But how stimulating it is! I'm so piss-full of ideas that after this last load of shit they've thrown at me I'll need a lifetime to write them all down.'
(Letter to Carl Larsson, 7 June 1883)

'I have discovered that I am not a realist. I write best when I hallucinate.'
(Letter to Jonas Lie, 24 May 1884)

'I sit and write like a sleepwalker, and must not be awakened, or it may stop in the middle.'
(Letter to Karl Otto Bonnier, 12 June 1884)

'I cannot rest, however much I might wish to. I have to write to eat, to keep my wife and children, and even apart from this I cannot stop. If I go on a train or whatever I do, my brain works ceaselessly, it grinds and grinds like a mill and I cannot make it stop. I find no rest till I have got it down on paper, but then something new starts at once and the same misery ensues. I write and write and do not even read through what I have written.'
(Strindberg, as recorded by Hélène Welinder, *Ögonvittnen, I* (Stockholm, 1959), p. 144)

'I am educating myself to become an atheist but am finding it horribly difficult.'
(Letter to Edvard Brandes, *c.* 12 June 1885)

'It seems to me that Strindberg's whole lifelong struggle had to be so difficult because at root it was a struggle against his inmost longings. He had been born into an age, and had been drawn into a way of thought, which suited his reason but not his general needs.'
(Karin Smirnoff, Strindberg's daughter, *Strindbergs första hustru* (Stockholm, 1926), p. 217)

'No one can stop me from setting my writings in Sweden. I know that country and its language best and hate it most.'
(Letter to Albert Bonnier, 22 Nov. 1885)

'I think I'm too much of an aristocrat amid all my demagogy to write for the masses.'

(Letter to Edvard Brandes, 9 June 1886)

'If only my brain and nerves could rest, but they chafe incessantly and the only rest I know is hard work. Hence I write too much.'

(Letter to Albert Bonnier, 3 Aug. 1886)

'. . . the theatre is a weapon . . . it's easier than novel-writing, once you get the knack. . . . Gondinet says that one needs to be a bit stupid to be able to write plays ['*Pour faire du théâtre, il faut être un peu bête*', E. Gondinet in *Le Figaro*, 22 Dec. 1885]. I think that's true of all creative writing. Once I started to think, my art went to pot.'

(Letter to Gustaf af Geijerstam, 4 Jan. 1887)

'That I have now [in *The Comrades*] portrayed a mean and dishonourable woman is no more unjust and unaesthetic than Ibsen's and the sisters' [i.e., the feminists'] scandalous attacks on the male sex. It is now becoming evident that woman is by nature mean and instinctively dishonest, though we ruttish cocks have not been able to see it; so, I have drawn a typical woman. . . . Actually my misogyny is purely theoretical, and I can't live a day without deluding myself that I warm my soul in the glow of their unconscious vegetable existence.'

(Letter to Edvard Brandes, 22 Jan. 1887)

'As a creative writer I blend fiction with reality, all my misogyny is theoretical, for I couldn't live without the company of women.'

(Letter to his brother Axel, 25 Feb. 1887)

'I can't work without the sound of children's voices.'

(Letter to Pehr Staaff, 5 Sept. 1887)

'Women, being small and foolish, and therefore evil . . . should be suppressed, like barbarians and thieves. They are useful only as ovary and womb, best of all as a cunt.'

(Letter to Verner von Heidenstam, 25 May 1888)

'Can you understand my misogyny? Which is only the reverse image of a terrible desire for the other sex.'

(Letter to Verner von Heidenstam, 13 Oct. 1888)

'Sometimes I feel the great agony of life, but sometimes, how my soul rejoices! The ring of tambourines and guitar music, jewels and expensive clothes . . . the wonders of our changing, colourful world fill me with an indescribable joy. . . . I seek loneliness because I love people too much. . . . I have to tear myself away from them, otherwise I can't work independently.'

(Interview in *Jämtlands-Posten*, 4 Sept. 1891)

'He writes without a pause, almost without stopping, does not even read over what he has written, let alone correct it.'

(Frida Uhl, Strindberg's second wife,
Marriage with Genius (London, 1937)

'Not to have found my destiny, that is the tragic thing. And this terrible discord between what I am and what I am supposed to be; the disproportion between my powers and what I achieve; my shame at unfulfilled obligations; the unjust hatred, persecution, chafing, the eternal harassment, the encroachment of material needs. I am sick, nervously sick, hovering between epileptic attacks of workomania and general paralysis.'

(Letter to Leopold Littmansson, 13 Aug. 1894)

'I avoided and neglected my fellow men, refused invitations, drove my friends from me. Silence and solitude encompassed me, the stillness of a desert, solemn, terrifying, in which I defiantly challenged the unseen Power to a wrestling match, body against body, soul against soul.'

(*Inferno*, trans. Mary Sandbach (London, 1962), p. 103)

'I too begin to feel an immense need to turn savage and create a new world.'

(Letter to Paul Gauguin, 1 Feb. 1895)

'In his reflections on the conflicts and disappointments of life, he repeatedly named Byron and Shelley. Gradually Byron and Shelley became "I", his voice became more bitter and harsher as he described the reverses and humiliations which he had endured as a human being and as an artist. . . . He told me that he had begun as a full-blooded idealist and had wanted "to bring down the stars from heaven so that men might see them and rejoice in them". . . . That he had given the best of himself and had found no understanding had wounded him so deeply that a great anger and desire for revenge had awoken in him, and he decided hereafter to leave the glittering stars of heaven as they were and instead pour out his hatred and spit out his anger at his contemporaries. . . . I felt as though I were strolling beside a wounded lion, a chained titan, who raged because, though conscious of his strength, he knew that he had always been a prisoner.'

(Esteri Kumlin, recalling Strindberg in 1895,
Ord och Bild (Stockholm, 1949))

'I have always felt a sympathy for that tortured self-torturing man, who offered himself to his own soul as Buddha offered himself to the famished tiger.'

(W.B. Yeats, *Autobiographies* (London, 1935), p. 539)

'My life has had the peculiarity that it unfolds like novels, without my really being able to say why. I don't meddle in other people's destinies. . . . But I have always been a kind of lime-twig; it attracts small birds, they finger my destiny, stick fast and then complain.'

(Letter to Torsten Hedlund, 26 June 1896)

'. . . I ended by becoming an occultist; that is, I received factual proof through the natural sciences that the soul was the all-important thing, the body only a transitory dress, that we are immortal, created, guided according to a natural plan, etc., all things long known. To confirm this I withdrew into isolation. . . .'

(Letter to Fritz Thaulow, *c*. 22 July 1896)

'I wonder where the grass grows where I may some time rest my weary bones, where the wild hunt of my Eumenides will cease.'

(Letter to Gustaf af Geijerstam, 12 May 1898)

'Do not use the word hallucination (nor even the word delirium) as though it expressed something unreal.'

(Letter to Gustaf Fröding, 5 June 1898)

'I have now put everything else aside to devote myself exclusively to writing for the theatre, so as to fulfil the promise I showed in my youth as a dramatist.'

(Letter to his daughter Greta, 26 Dec. 1898)

[*On the rejection of his early play* Master Olof, *which had deflected him from the theatre at a critical stage in his career.*] 'My life is a cripple lacking a foot of spine. The years between twenty and thirty are missing; the best years. . . . Imagine yourself painting enormous canvases which never get accepted for exhibition but which you must roll up and carry to the attic where they must lie until they grow old-fashioned. That is what I have had to do repeatedly.'

(Letter to Carl Larsson, 24 Jan. 1889)

'E. von Hartmann says that love is a farce invented by nature to fool men and women into propagating their species. Life revolts me and always has done so. Everything is worthless. . . . When I was immoral, I was abused, and when I was moral I was abused even more. People are not born evil but life makes them evil. So life cannot be an education, nor a chastisement (which improves), but only an evil.'

(Strindberg's diary, 6 Sept. 1901)

'A work of art should be a little careless, imperfect like any natural growth, where not a crystal is perfect, not a plant lacks its defective leaf. As with Shakespeare.'

(Letter to Emil Schering, 13 May 1902)

'His daily walks from 7 to 9 a.m. were, strictly speaking, the only time he took fresh air. He rose at 6.30, made his own coffee in a Russian machine, then walked to Djurgården. He told me that during these walks he planned his day's work. . . . On returning home, he sat down immediately at his desk, charged with ideas. While he wrote, he chain-smoked Finnish cigarettes. As is known, he usually had the shape of what he was to write, and the dialogue, ready in his head, so that there are very few changes in his manuscripts. . . . He would read in the afternoon, preparing his next day's work, but he never wrote then.'

(Harriet Bosse, Strindberg's third wife,
Strindbergs brev till Harriet Bosse (Stockholm, 1932), p. 78-9)

'I feel that I owe it to the actors to watch a performance, from an invisible position, on an evening when no one in the theatre knows I am there, and although it is a torture to me to see my shadows and hear my words, I shall do my duty. On the other hand, I enjoy socializing in small groups, in informal dress and without ceremony. . . . Everything public I hate, quite pathologically.'

(Letter to Emil Schering, 22 Oct. 1902)

'Life is so cynical that only a swine can be happy in it. And anyone who can see our ugly life as beautiful is a swine. Life must be a punishment! A hell; for some a purgatory, for none a Paradise. We are forced to do evil and torment our fellow creatures. It is all sham and delusion, lies, infidelity, falsehood, farce. "My dear friend" should read "my worst enemy". "My beloved" should read "my hated".'

(Strindberg's diary, 3 Sept. 1904)

'My disharmonies rend me. Loneliness forces me to seek company, but after each meeting, even the best, I withdraw wounded and find myself more and more turned in on myself; am ashamed without cause, suffer remorse without having done anything, am disgusted with myself without knowing why. I strive upwards but go down; want to do so much good, but behave so badly; my old self strives against my new; I want to see life as beautiful, but it is not beautiful, only nature is beautiful; I pity people but I cannot respect them, cannot love them, I know them through myself. I find my only comfort now in Buddha who says plainly that life is a phanthasma, an illusion, the truth of which we shall see in another life. My hope and my future lie on the other side, that is why life is so difficult for me to live. . . . Wife, children, and home were the best; a stern school, but the only protection against bad influences; without this protection I drift, fall into the hands of anyone; loneliness is not bad, but there I am faced by my stern chastising self, which scourges me.'

(Letter to Harriet Bosse, 4 Oct. 1905)

'When I return from my morning walk I am charged like an electric machine. After putting on a dry shirt, for I get very hot when walking, I sit down at this desk. As soon as I have pen and paper ready it starts to flow. The words pour forth and my pen has to work at full pressure to get it all down. After a few minutes I have the feeling that I am hovering freely in space. It is as though a higher will than mine causes the pen to glide across the paper and write words that seem to me to come from without.'

(Strindberg, reported by Gustaf Uddgren, in
Andra boken om Strindberg (Gothenburg, 1912), p. 136)

'. . . a handsome baby, saint, lion – a queer mixture . . . the fine curve of his back, more like that of a man of twenty than one of sixty, and which he emphasized by putting his hands in his jacket pockets.'

(Edward Gordon Craig,
in a radio talk broadcast in London in 1956)

'After sixty years of torture I pray to God to be allowed to depart from life. The little joy there was was illusory or false. Work was the only thing! but that was largely wasted; or useless, or harmful. Wife, children, home, were all a mockery. The only thing that gave me an illusion of happiness was drink. So I drank! It also mollified the agony of existence. It made my torpid mind alert and intelligent; sometimes in youth, it stilled my hunger. . . . Women gave me a great illusion of happiness which, however, immediately evaporated, and revealed its true nature. The first two left no memories behind them, only a keen loathing. In the last there was something from a higher sphere, but mixed with so much that was evil and ugly. Yet I remember her often very beautifully, though most of it was false. When my children were small they gave me the purest joy. But that soon vanished. . . .'

(Strindberg's diary, 13 June 1908)

'It is as though a mad soul were seated in the wrong body – I have always felt this.'

(Letter to Nils Andersson, 12 June 1911)

'One has to go abroad to learn what Strindberg really means in Europe. During these last years I have found that in Germany, Austria, Russia, and fashionable circles in France, he is rated as comparable to Ibsen and is overshadowed only by Tolstoy. . . .

Wherever I went in Europe his name was the same fire on the tongues of the young as Ibsen's once was. People in Sweden do not seem to know this.'

(Herman Bang, the Danish writer, in interviews published in the Stockholm newspapers *Dagens Nyheter* and *Svenska Dagbladet*, 17 Oct. 1911, seven months before Strindberg's death)

'That greatest genius of all modern dramatists.'

(Eugene O'Neill, quoted in Louis Shaeffer, *O'Neill, Son and Artist* (London, 1974), p. 124)

'Strindberg, Strindberg, Strindberg, the greatest of them all.'

(Sean O'Casey, in a letter to Robert Loraine, Aug. 1927, after seeing the latter in *The Father*, in *The Letters of Sean O'Casey, 1910-1954, I*, ed. David Krause, (New York, 1975), p. 217)

'Strindberg has been the European writer who has been closest to me, the one who has most strongly inspired my thoughts and emotions. Every book he wrote spurred one to argue with him, to contradict him, every book deepened and strengthened one's love of and respect for him. ... To light the way for those who wandered in the perplexities of darkness, and show the path to understanding and freedom, he tore the heart from his breast, set it on fire and carried it as a torch to lead mankind.'

(Maxim Gorki, quoted in Walter Berendsohn, *Strindbergs sista levnadsår* (Stockholm, 1948), p. 171)

'He is among the greatest of the great.'

(Bernard Shaw, quoted in *Adam*, Strindberg centenary issue (London, 1949), p. 1)

a: Primary Sources
Translations

Michael Meyer, trans. Strindberg: *The Plays, I-II*
(London: Secker and Warburg, 1964, 1975). These
volumes contain: (I) *The Father*, Miss Julie*,
Creditors, The Stronger*, Playing with Fire, Erik
the Fourteenth, Storm, The Ghost Sonata**; (II) *To
Damascus I-III, Easter, The Dance of Death I-II*,
The Virgin Bride, A Dream Play** (plays marked
with an asterisk are also available in two Methuen
paperbacks: *Strindberg Plays: One and Plays: Two*).
Mary Sandbach, transl. *Inferno* and *From an Occult
Diary* (London: Hutchinson, 1962, Secker & Warburg,
1965, issued in a single volume by Penguin, 1979).
Mary Sandbach, trans. *Getting Married* (London:
Gollancz, 1972; Quartet paperback, 1977).
Mary Sandbach, trans. *By the Open Sea* (London:
Secker and Warburg, 1984).
Evert Sprinchorn, trans. *The Son of a Servant* (New
York: Anchor, 1966).

b: Secondary Sources
Full-length Studies

Frida Strindberg, *Marriage with Genius*. London: Cape,
1937.
Adam (London). Strindberg centenary issue, 1949.
Eric O. Johannesson, *The Novels of August Strindberg*.
Berkeley: University of California Press, 1968.
Martin Lamm, *August Strindberg*, trans. Harry
G. Carlson. New York: Blom, 1971.
Gunnar Brandell, *Strindberg in Inferno*, trans. Barry
Jacobs. Cambridge, Mass.: Harvard University Press,
1974.
Evert Sprinchorn, *Strindberg as Dramatist*. New Haven
and London: Yale University Press, 1982.
Harry G. Carlson, *Strindberg and the Poetry of Myth*.
Berkeley: University of California Press, 1982.
Michael Meyer, *Strindberg: a Biography*. London and
New York: Secker and Warburg and Random House,
1985.

A Note on Strindberg Criticism

The press notices of Strindberg productions in Britain, like those in Sweden and elsewhere, contain a rich vein of ridicule. On the occasion of the British premiere of *The Father* in 1911, the *Times* dismissed him as 'extraordinarily naïve in some of his dramatic processes', and the *Academy* asked: 'Why use the theatre for unrelieved depression and brutal aspects of human nature and relationships exploited in the name of art?'

One of the first British writers to appreciate Strindberg's stature was Rupert Brooke. 'There are two things about him that are important', Brooke wrote in the *Cambridge Magazine* (11 Oct. 1913), 'his significance and position in the waves and currents of the thought of his time, and the power and genius of a few of his plays. . . . What is most to be hoped for from his influence is an infusion of power into the drama. His range of characters may be rather limited; but . . . Strindberg saw people, in their general nature, something as they really are, and not as the rationally moved, explanatory puppets of other drama. When lovers first kiss, it is reported, they feel as if, almost physically, two gigantic invisible hands were softly, irresistibly pressing their heads together. By such vast and uncomprehended compulsion are Strindberg's people, in part, moved . . . by forces we can never quite understand.'

But complaints were more common than praise over the next forty years. As late as 1962, in a book entitled *The Drama of Ibsen and Strindberg*, a Cambridge don, F.L. Lucas, found *The Father* 'unredeemably ugly . . . like a visit to a gloomy cavern full of flickering bats – not unimpressive, but repulsive; a glimpse of Hell, that shows only things to shun', and summarized *Miss Julie* as a play 'about a lout and a trollop. . . . Is it very civilized to enjoy the anguish of this wretched girl, like *tricoteuses* knitting around the guillotine?' *The Ghost Sonata* Lucas dismissed as 'odious, diseased and corrupting', while the two parts of *The Dance of Death* 'would be atrocious, were they not ridiculous. . . . This nasty play. . . . Such homes may really exist; though their occupants would be better in mental ones.'

Critical opinion has now come to accept Strindberg as one of the great masters of tragedy. On 3 January 1976 in *The Spectator*, John Mortimer noted that Strindberg was the first dramatist not to have presented himself as 'the reasonable man of moderation, the sort of character of sterling common sense that his audience was flattered into believing it also represented. . . . The movement of modern drama has been, surely, a flight from reason into the terrifying abyss of Beckett, or the irrational fears of Pinter. John Osborne's . . . Jimmy Porter and Archie Rice are not reasonable men. They live in a different world from Shakespeare and Montaigne; their anger is at best an expression of the hopelessly absurd facts of existence, at worst a scream of paranoia. They are in Strindberg's world. . . . He found the joy of life in its "cruel and mighty conflicts", and the exhilaration his best work brings is not that it is intelligent (like much of life, it is totally absurd), but that it is absolutely true. It is by facing the irrational truth of existence that the writer and his characters achieve such peace as they ever know. . . . [His] is not the voice of reason; but it is the true voice of experience hardly won, and it is the voice of modern drama.'